THE SOCIOLOGY OF
SHOPLIFTING

PRAEGER SERIES IN CRIMINOLOGY AND CRIME CONTROL POLICY

Steven A. Egger, Series Editor

Power, Ideology, and the War on Drugs: Nothing Succeeds Like Failure
Cristina Jacqueline Johns

The Sociology of Shoplifting: Boosters and Snitches Today
Lloyd W. Klemke

The Sociology of
SHOPLIFTING

Boosters and Snitches Today

LLOYD W. KLEMKE

Praeger series in Criminology and Crime Control Policy
STEVEN A. EGGER, SERIES EDITOR

Westport, Connecticut
London

Library of Congress Cataloging-in-Publication Data

Klemke, Lloyd W.
    The sociology of shoplifting : boosters and snitches today / Lloyd
W. Klemke.
        p.   cm. — (Praeger series in criminology and crime control
policy)
    Includes bibliographical references and index.
    ISBN 0–275–94108–6 (alk. paper)
    1. Shoplifting—United States. I. Title. II. Series.
HV6658.K54   1992
364.1'62—dc20   91–45609

British Library Cataloguing in Publication Data is available.

Library of Congress Catalog Card Number: 91–45609
ISBN: 0-275-94108-6

First published in 1992

Praeger Publishers, 88 Post Road West, Westport, CT 06881
An imprint of Greenwood Publishing Group, Inc.

Printed in the United States of America

∞™

The paper used in this book complies with the
Permanent Paper Standard issued by the National
Information Standards Organization (Z39.48–1984).

10 9 8 7 6 5 4 3 2 1

Copyright Acknowledgments

The author and publisher are grateful to the following for allowing use of their material:

"A Face-Off With Racism." *U.S. News & World Report*, August 22, 1988. Copyright, Aug. 22, 1988, U.S. News & World Report. Used by permission.

Excerpts from Charles E. Faupel and Gregory S. Kowalski. 1990. "Heroin Use, Crime, and the Main Hustle." *Deviant Behavior* 11(1): 9. Used by permission.

Excerpts from Bruce D. Johnson et al. 1985. *Taking Care of Business: The Economics of Crime by Heroin Users*. Lexington, Mass.: Lexington Books. Used by permission.

Excerpts from Lloyd W. Klemke. 1978. "Reassessment of the Adolescent Crime Model." *California Sociologist* 1, 2 (Summer): 184. Used by permission.

Excerpts from Henry Mayhew. 1968. *London Labour and the London Poor*. Minola, N.Y.: Dover Publcations. Used by permission.

Excerpts from *Manny: A Criminal Addict's Story* by Richard P. Rettig et al. Copyright © 1977 by Harper & Row, Publishers, Inc. Reprinted by permission of HarperCollins Publishers.

Excerpts from Clifford R. Shaw. 1931. *The Natural History of a Delinquent Career*. Chicago: University of Chicago Press. Used by permission.

Excerpts from Frederick M. Thrasher. 1927. *The Gang; A Study of 1,313 Gangs*. Chicago: University of Chicago Press. Used by permission.

CONTENTS

TABLES

SERIES FOREWORD

Klemke's analysis of shoplifting is a long overdue contribution to the literature on crime and deviance. It has been almost thirty years since Cameron published her monograph on shoplifting. Since then few research efforts have successfully examined this phenomenon in any great detail. The research questions that Klemke answers in *The Sociology of Shoplifting: Boosters and Snitches Today*, will be of special interest to researchers and theorists in the sociology of deviance as well as to the retail community and to security administrators.

As Klemke notes throughout his work, not a great deal of attention has been paid by the research community to the problems of shoplifting. This is indeed unfortunate, given the fact that shoplifting is a significant part of official delinquency and is a crime that represents a real "epidemic" increase during the last two decades. Also, this property crime results in tremendous financial losses for the retail community as Klemke describes throughout the book with up-to-date figures and analysis.

In addition to presenting a concise synthesis of the diverse literature on shoplifting, Klemke provides a clear contemporary assessment of the consensus, controversy, and future direction of research into this phenomenon. Klemke presents his qualitative analysis of shoplifting in chapter two, followed by a quantitative analysis in chapter three. Rich ethnographic and historical accounts of this phenomenon precede the empirical and more traditional descriptions that follow. Chapter four provides an exhaustive analysis of the various typologies of shoplifting and shoplifters.

Chapter five explores the various behavioral theories used to explain shoplifting. Chapter six examines societal response to the problem of shoplifting. Here the response in the retail industry is described followed by the legal system's response. Deterrence as well as prevention strategies are critically reviewed here. The final chapter presents the reader with a succinct overview of the author's work.

Klemke presents a careful and insightful update to the pioneering work of Cameron. This effort alone has provided a valuable monograph. More importantly, Klemke's analysis and research into the phenomenon of shoplifting has resulted in a "deviance vulnerability-shoplifting attraction" theoretical framework, which he presents in preliminary form for the reader. The development of this preliminary construct will undoubtedly stimulate further research into the theory of shoplifting.

As Series Editor, my original expectation for this monograph has been greatly exceeded. I sincerely hope readers of this work will recognize the value of Lloyd Klemke's efforts to the field of criminology, crime control, and the sociology of deviance.

Steven A. Egger
Series Editor

ACKNOWLEDGMENTS

The process of writing a book begins long before the first word is put to paper (or word processor). Special thanks are due to several mentors who increased my initial interest in the study of deviance. They are Lewis Yablonsky, Bernard A. Thorsell, Walter E. Schafer, and Kenneth Polk. During the writing of the book I relied on a number of key reviewers and colleagues to improve the quality of my efforts. John A. Velke, Director of Security for a multi-state department store, provided access to data, and read and commented on much of the manuscript. Bernard A. Thorsell closely read and fine-tuned most of the manuscript. Gary Tiedeman forewarned me of his notoriously active red pencil. Fortunately, I was not intimidated, and the manuscript has been significantly improved both substantively and in its readability as a result of his suggestions. Finally, Jon Hendricks, an outstanding gerontologist, graciously shared his vast experience in writing with me. He painstakingly read, critiqued, and edited the manuscript. He was also a constant source of support and encouragement for this project. My deep appreciation is extended for the unique contributions provided by each of these reviewers.

Special thanks are also due to Steven Eggers, Anne Kiefer, and Talvi Leav of Praeger for their support and assistance in bringing this publication to print. Carol Peck provided able secretarial assistance and extricated me from numerous predicaments encountered with my computer. I am also indebted to the individuals who have shared their shoplifting experiences with me over the years. Finally, my family has been a constant source of support for this endeavor, much beyond what can be fully acknowledged on paper. My wife, Tina, has abundantly and lovingly shared her life with me; my son, Ken, provided welcomed and needed tennis and fly-fishing therapy trips; and my daughter, Cammy, has always been a special person!

1

AN INTRODUCTION TO THE STUDY OF SHOPLIFTING

She rounded the corner into the aisle that had the beer and chilled wine and almost crashed into a man holding open the flap of his parka, stuffing an inside pocket with what looked like a bottle of champagne. He was so thin and the jacket so big that when he jerked it across his chest, the bottle was swallowed up—except for a barely discernible curve of glass against nylon, invisible.

Ellen Lesser,
The Shoplifter's Apprentice (p. 9)

One day my wife and I were shopping at a mall in a neighboring community. During the day our paths intersected a number of times with a Native American family (husband, wife, a girl about ten years old, and a younger boy). After a long day of shopping, I finally persuaded my wife that we should head for home. As we strolled through the parking lot, the Native American family was also walking from the mall. Coincidentally, their car was parked within a few spaces of our car. Before we reached our car, I noticed another shopper some distance behind the family. What especially caught my attention was the behavior of this person, who appeared to be talking to the backpack that he was carrying. Given the community where we were shopping, I was not too surprised to encounter some unusual folks. Moments later, just as the family reached their car, a security vehicle came zooming down the lane and another sped in from the opposite direction, completely blocking in their car. The eccentric "talking-to-a-backpack-shopper," who had transformed into a security officer, began to interrogate the concerned family. The shopping bags that they were carrying and packages already in the car and trunk were examined and confiscated. Soon, the now sullen family was escorted back into the formerly enticing mall.

I was left wondering about what had transpired during that family's shopping trip to the mall. How much had been shoplifted? Who was involved? Was it one of the adults or the children, or was it a family activity? Had they done this before? What were the reasons behind the shoplifting? Did their ethnic background play any role in their being suspected, watched, and eventually apprehended by a strong contingent of security personnel? How would this experience impact on their lives? Would any of them ever shoplift in the future?

Besides the incident just described, I can recall only one time that I observed a shoplifting incident occur. One day while I was shopping at a table of sale clothing, two young teenage girls began to browse through the items close to me. After a short time, I heard one of the girls whisper encouragement to her friend to "Go ahead, take it!" Soon an item disappeared under a coat. Being a sociologist versed in unobtrusive observation, I justified not doing anything that might alter the natural flow of events. My inaction was not unique, as several field experimental studies (utilizing confederate "shoplifters" who stole something in view of a shopper) have confirmed that *most* shoppers do not intervene or report an observed incident to store personnel (Steffensmeier and Terry, 1973; Gelfand et al., 1973).

On a more personal note, my own "career" in shoplifting began and ended in my childhood years, similar to that of many other people. I can recall periodically (15 to 20 times) succumbing to the temptation of alluring candies, toys, and fishing gear between the ages of about 8 and 12. Guilt and fear of being detected eventually aborted further development of this budding deviant career.

I suspect that I am typical of many people in our society who have experienced only limited personal involvement with shoplifting but still are intrigued by this type of behavior. This, then, presents an interesting quandry. Given the high level of interest and fascination with the phenomenon of shoplifting, why has it not commanded more attention from social scientists? Sociologists have contributed only modest research efforts toward discovering the basic descriptive patterns of this type of crime. Likewise, the search for explanations of shoplifting has generated some interesting beginnings, but much remains to be done. To date, there has only been one significant American sociological monograph devoted to shoplifting. Mary Owen Cameron's *The Booster and the Snitch* (1964) has become a mini-classic due to her resourceful and engaging analysis. Its status has also been elevated because there have been only a few competing publications on the topic. One of these, by a British sociologist, is Daniel Murphy's (1986) book *Customers and Thieves*. This is a limited but interesting ethnographic look at shoplifting in England.

More recently, Elaine Abelson's *When Ladies Go A-Thieving* (1989b) has helped to stimulate interest. Her insightful historical analysis of shoplifting from the mid-1800s to the early 1900s reveals how productive the analysis of shoplifting can be. Besides these volumes, most of the sociological research on shoplifting is found in articles scattered throughout professional journals.

While the social science literature is rather modest, considerable public attention has been devoted to shoplifting. Articles on shoplifting appear regularly in mass media magazines and newspapers (e.g., Tooley, 1989; Tsiantar, 1989). They frequently highlight the seriousness of the problem, famous personalities apprehended for shoplifting (e.g., beauty queens, politicians, and other celebrities), or interesting types of shoplifters (e.g., middle-class housewives or the elderly). Moralistic themes are often developed, showing how lives have been traumatized by the embarrassment of a shoplifting arrest. For example, Jimmy Smits, the popular star of the TV series "L.A. Law," described in *Parade* (Buchalter, 1990) how "awful he felt" after his parents found out that he had been caught shoplifting model airplane parts. It also does not take a genius level of intelligence to foresee the professional damage that may be triggered when a celebrity is caught shoplifting. For example, it was not long after the Associated Press revealed that National League umpire Bob Engle had been charged with shoplifting large numbers of baseball cards from two stores that he resigned from his position (*Corvallis Gazette-Times*, 1990). These types of personal interest articles provide emotionally engaging "morality lessons" to the public to refrain from shoplifting.

Another source of information on shoplifting is the extensive literature in trade publications and professional journals targeted to the retail business community and the security industry. Good overviews of the type of analysis characterizing this literature can be found in *Shoplifting and Shrinkage Protection for Stores* by Loren Edwards (1970), *Combatting Retail Theft: Programs and Strategies* by Terry Baumer and Dennis Rosenbaum (1984), and *Shoplifting: The Antishoplifting Guidebook* by Kathleen Farrell (1985). Overall, this literature highlights research on patterns and trends in shoplifting and extensive discussions about store security issues and practices. Most of these sources provide advice and/or promote various preventive-deterrent strategies or technological innovations aimed at reducing shoplifting. They are usually written by security personnel and are based on their years of experience in dealing with shoplifters. Their assertions are often not backed up with systematically collected data. Still, their extensive first-hand experience demands that they be considered as a source for trends and hypotheses that can be explored and tested by social science researchers.

My own research on shoplifting began with a self-report study of juvenile shoplifters (Klemke, 1978a; 1978b; 1982a; 1982b). More recently

I have reviewed the extant literature on shoplifting. The material runs the gamut of the social sciences, retail trade magazines, professional business journals, security-oriented magazines, and mass media publications. I have also collected store apprehension data from several retail establishments.

To gain insight into shoplifting I have conducted unstructured interviews with small samples of shoplifters and store security personnel. In addition, questionnaires were administered to two classes of college students. Overall, 56 percent of the 165 respondents had shoplifted. Data were obtained on their shoplifting involvements, motives, and attitudes. Adopting a strategy used by Jack Katz (1988), I also asked the respondents to describe what they were doing, thinking, and feeling during their most memorable, or most recent, shoplifting experience. Because it was a convenience sample I will report only suggestive statistics and illustrative quotes from this exploratory study. More important, it has provided one more window through which to view the phenomenon of shoplifting. Collectively, these research experiences and the literature review have led me to the conclusion that a contemporary analysis that summarizes, synthesizes, and critically reviews the accumulating work on shoplifting is long overdue.

GOALS AND FOCUS OF THIS BOOK

The intent of this book is to provide an analysis of what is currently known about shoplifters and shoplifting for several key audiences. It is hoped that researchers and theorists in the sociology of deviance-crime areas will find this a useful addition to the literature. It is also designed to help instruct students, because it explores many basic issues and provides a model of how sociologists approach the study of crime and deviance. Finally, to the degree that it adds to our understanding of shoplifters and shoplifting, it will also be valuable to the retail community and, more specifically, to security personnel who must deal with the shoplifting phenomenon.

The analysis will cover an extensive range of the methodological approaches and theoretical issues found in the sociology of deviance-crime literature. Three simple questions will structure the discussion. They are: (1) Who shoplifts and how do they do it? (the descriptive question); (2) Why do they shoplift? (the etiological question); and (3) How do store personnel and the legal system deal with shoplifters? (the prevention-detection-deterrence question). These are the classic questions that dominate the sociology of deviance literature. Much of the existing research on shoplifting is scattered in many different sources and buried within studies devoted to other topics. Therefore, a considerable effort will be devoted to gathering this material (interviews, self-report data, store record statistics, etc.) together in one source. Analysis of the research will seek to identify the areas where consensus and confidence already exists. Particular attention will be paid to pinpointing the gaps in our knowledge, as well as the areas of controversy and debate that continue to perplex students of shoplifting. This contemporary assessment will also point to directions for future research.

WHY THERE IS ONLY LIMITED SOCIOLOGICAL RESEARCH ON SHOPLIFTING

It is interesting and instructive to look at the reasons why there has been only modest sociological interest in this fascinating type of crime. Why, for example, do most deviance and criminology texts virtually ignore shoplifting? If it is mentioned at all, it is usually only in a perfunctory reference to Cameron's study. One reason for the minimal coverage may be the lack of significant studies on shoplifting. While there is some truth to this possibility, I would argue that there is a modest and respectable core of studies that, for various reasons, has not attracted a great deal of attention.

Another reason for the lack of interest may be the trend to look at crime and delinquency as a *general* phenomenon instead of looking at *specific* types of crime. Delinquency researchers, in particular, have established that most delinquents are involved in a wide variety of delinquent acts and rarely specialize in one type of delinquency. This tends to discourage researchers from focusing on a single type of deviance. As a result, unique insights that apply to particular types of deviance are overlooked.

Yet another possible reason for the lack of attention may be that the research community has not taken seriously the retail community's claim that shoplifting constitutes a major problem. Even efforts to mobilize public sympathy with media campaigns like STEM (Shoplifters Take Everybody's Money) have not generated much concern. Sociologists have analyzed the importance of "claims-making" and mobilization efforts that are necessary to transform a potential social problem into a bona fide social problem (Best, 1987; Gusfield, 1989). Specific crimes, for example, have become "hot" topics for the general public. Social scientists have also jumped on various social problem bandwagons, particularly when research funding has been dangled in front of them. Thus, we have seen significant bursts of interest and research on missing children, domestic violence, sex abuse, gangs, serial killers, and drug abuse. Shoplifting, however, has rarely "caught on" among social science researchers as a worthy social problem. This may be due to the fact that shoplifting does not result in eye-catching "body counts" or astronomical dollar losses being generated by *individual* shoplifters.

Table 1.1
Mean Perceived Seriousness of Selected Offenses

Offense Description	Mean Seriousness Score
Robbing a store and killing two employees	9.87
A father sexually abusing his teenage daughter	9.36
Ten high school boys beating up a classmate	7.63
Breaking into a house and stealing a TV set	6.69
Shoplifting merchandise worth $600 from a store	6.63
Writing a bad check for $350 to a store	5.78
Breaking into a parking meter and stealing $2	4.71
Painting obscenities on a highway billboard	3.92
Shoplifting a pair of socks from a store	3.13
Trespassing in a railroad yard	2.37

Source: Adapted from Table 1 in Mark Warr (1989), "What Is the Perceived Seriousness of Crimes?" (*Criminology* 27(4): 801).

Without sensational evidence of cataclysmic harm to foster and fuel public concern, most people consider shoplifting to be an interesting but not a very serious type of crime.

Several sociologists have verified the lack of concern about shoplifting by exploring how citizens rate the seriousness of various criminal acts (Rossi et al., 1974; *Bureau of Justice Statistics*, 1984; Warr, 1989). In these studies random samples of citizens were asked to make judgments about the seriousness of various types of criminal acts. In all cases, shoplifting small items such as a book or pair of socks was rated very low in seriousness. However, when the item shoplifted was a diamond ring or merchandise worth $600, then citizens gave this type of act a medium degree of seriousness score similar to a traditional type of crime like burglary. These patterns are evident in Table 1.1, which shows a partial set of illustrative data from Warr's (1989) recent study of Dallas residents. His respondents were asked to judge the seriousness of various criminal acts on a ten-point scale, with 0 being the least serious and 10 being the most serious. His results confirm that most people do not think that the shoplifting of inexpensive items, which is the most frequent type of shoplifting, is a very serious matter.[1]

Finally, a significant segment of citizens and social scientists hold blatant anti-business attitudes that reduce their sympathy for the problems of retail establishments. Sociologists, for example, are currently more inclined to write books like *Elite Deviance* (Simon and Eitzen, 1982), *Corporate and Government Deviance* (Erman and Lundman, 1987), and

Corporate Violence (Hills, 1987) than (the imaginary) *Ripping Off the Rich Merchant*. I strongly agree that major social harm is done by elite deviants and that it must be analyzed and publicized. It is, however, only fair and reasonable that we should also examine the victimization of the business community in order to cover the full spectrum of deviance.[2]

WHY MORE RESEARCH ON SHOPLIFTING IS WARRANTED

Developing the case for increasing the scholarly research on shoplifting is not very difficult. Many different types of statistics can be marshalled to document the scope of the shoplifting problem.[3] For example, a report on the juvenile court records of ten states shows that shoplifting is a significant part of the official delinquency problem. It concludes that (1) shoplifting was the most common offense for which youth under age 15 were referred to court; and (2) shoplifting was the most common offense for female youth (Nimick, 1990).

Another source of official data, the Federal Bureau of Investigation's (FBI) annual *Uniform Crime Reports*, presents statistics on shoplifting as one type of larceny. This information is based on offenses *known to the police* and covers all age groups. Store personnel, however, frequently report only the loss of expensive items to the police. Likewise, they report and pass on only *some* of the apprehended suspects (the most important factor probably being the dollar value of the shoplifted items) to the police. Therefore, *Uniform Crime Reports* data, like the juvenile court data, represent a very minimal indicator of the actual amount of shoplifting activity. This resource also presents very little specific data (i.e., sex or age breakdowns) about shoplifting. Table 1.2 shows the number of shoplifting incidents reported to the police in recent years. As is apparent, shoplifting known to the police has dramatically increased from 349,283 incidents in 1973 to 1,059,765 in 1989.[4] Remember, however, that this represents only the tip of the shoplifting iceberg, because most shoplifting is not detected by store personnel. Furthermore, all of what is detected by store personnel may not be reported to the police.

The large, approximately 300 percent increase in shoplifting since 1973 may represent a real "epidemic" increase in shoplifting activity and/or may simply indicate that there have been significant changes in detection and reporting practices by store personnel. Only one study provides national data on shoplifting trends. Fortunately, it covers most of the years shown in Table 1.2. This is the *Monitoring the Future* study of self-report data collected annually from a large national sample of high school seniors (Johnston et al., 1977–1986). Because it encompasses only one age group and samples individuals who were still in school, the generalizability of the findings is limited. Still, it provides a unique data set

Table 1.2
Number of Shoplifting Thefts Known to Police for Recent Years in the United States

Year	Total Number of Shoplifting Thefts
1973	349,283
1974	450,096
1975	532,656
1976	579,978
1977	607,712
1978	624,387
1979	688,494
1980	744,049
1981	741,800
1982	775,065
1983	804,051
1984	766,920
1985	903,242
1986	1,023,447
1987	1,027,322
1988	982,555
1989	1,059,765

Source: Derived from statistics in Timothy J. Flanagan and Kathleen Maguire, eds. (1990) *Sourcebook of Criminal Justice Statistics—1989* (Washington, D.C.: U.S. Government Printing Office), 394; and Kathleen Maguire and Timothy J. Flanagan, eds. (1991), *Sourcebook of Criminal Justice Statistics—1990* (Washington, D.C.: U.S. Government Printing Office), 376.

that reveals trends for a significant segment of the population. Data from this study challenge the view that shoplifting has been increasing dramatically. In fact, the *Monitoring the Future* data show that there has been virtually no change in shoplifting activity between 1977 and 1988 (Flanagan and Maguire, 1988: 339). The pattern for 1977 (30.2% reported shoplifting during the last year) is nearly identical to that reported for 1988 (30.4%). At no time between 1977 and 1988 was there more than a four-point fluctuation in the percentage reporting recent shoplifting activity. Keeping in mind the sample limitations, this study strongly suggests that there has not been a recent epidemic of shoplifting. Therefore, the increase shown in FBI data is more likely to be a product of changes in apprehension and reporting practices than a real increase in shoplifting behavior.

The average financial value of each shoplifting incident increased from

$32 in 1974 to $102 in 1989 (Federal Bureau of Investigation, 1975; 1990). As stores usually report only expensive shoplifting incidents to the police, this statistic greatly exaggerates the financial value of a "typical" shoplifting theft. Altogether, the FBI statistics show that a total of $120,211,520 in merchandise was shoplifted in 1988. This does not constitute a total loss to retail establishments, however, as a considerable amount is recovered when apprehensions are made. Unfortunately, the FBI does not supply this statistic. It is available for Oregon, where 40.3 percent of the $1.4 million in shoplifting losses known to the police for 1988 was recovered (Oregon Law Enforcement Data System, 1989). Finally, the retail community has increasingly resorted to civil recovery procedures to extract financial restitution from apprehended shoplifters. Thirty-one states make some provision for recovering financial costs from shoplifters (*Chain Store Age Executive*, 1988). California merchants, for example, can collect up to $500 from an apprehended shoplifter. States and stores that utilize this legal process can significantly reduce the total cost of shoplifting losses.

Because of the inherent problems with *Uniform Crime Reports* data, researchers have utilized other techniques to obtain more detailed and accurate information. Numerous social scientists and security personnel have examined store apprehension statistics. These statistics will be extensively described and evaluated in Chapter 3. For the present, it is sufficient to note that store apprehension data present much larger numbers on how much shoplifting activity is taking place than are recorded in the *Uniform Crime Reports*.

The following estimates of shoplifting losses, derived from store apprehension data, run into the billions of dollars. One estimate comes from the data collected by Commercial Services Systems (Griffin, 1988). For 25 years this organization has generated an annual report on data collected from supermarkets (391 stores in 1987) in southern California. Based on their experience, the average value of merchandise recovered from a supermarket store shoplifting apprehension in 1987 was $11.19. Using a conservative estimate of only nine shoplifting thefts a day per supermarket (for small grocery stores and convenience stores, they halve the number of thefts and the dollar value lost), multiplied by the number of days and the number of stores, they generate an estimate of $2,203,454,286 in shoplifting loss for all U.S. grocery stores in 1987.

One of the largest estimates, made by Warren A. French (French, Crask, and Mader, 1984), for the now defunct National Coalition to Prevent Shoplifting, set the cost of shoplifting for 1981 at $31 billion. This appears to be an exaggerated figure. Peter D. Berlin, who offers one of the sophisticated consulting services for retailers, places the 1987 total inventory shrinkage (this includes internal theft, computing and accounting errors, and shoplifting) at $13.5 billion (Barmash, 1988). Experts from three different national organizations estimate that retail shrinkage losses can be attributed to the following: 40–50 percent due to employee theft, 25–30 percent due to shoplifting, and 15–30 percent due to accounting errors (Carlson, 1984). Other experts, particularly store executives, consider shoplifting to be a bigger problem than employee theft and assign their security personnel to focus primarily on the shoplifting problem (Murphy, 1986). Even though precise figures of the cost of shoplifting are not available (and probably never will be), there is no doubt that shoplifting does impose a serious economic burden on retail establishments (Fisher, 1991). Ultimately, non-shoplifting consumers pay more for their purchases to cover the shrinkage losses and the costs of store security.

While the figures present alarming numbers, store apprehension statistics are, obviously, based only on those who get caught! Because many individuals are adept shoplifters and many stores have minimal detection efforts, most shoplifters do *not* get caught. Several studies report estimates that less than 1 percent of all shoplifters end up being apprehended (Blankenburg, 1976; Baumer and Rosenbaum, 1984). To obtain a more accurate profile of shoplifters, researchers have resorted to observational or self-report research methods.

Observational studies offer a relatively simple and potentially valuable means of expanding our knowledge of the scope of shoplifting behavior. Unlike many types of deviance (e.g., rape, burglary, domestic abuse, etc.) shoplifting occurs in public places, making it amenable to observational research. There are, however, questions about (1) the ability of observers to be in a position to detect all acts of shoplifting; and (2) whether having observers shadowing customers, even though attempting to remain unobtrusive, could serve as an inhibitor of potential shoplifting activity. Data from three observational studies have been collected and summarized by Abigale Buckle and David Farrington (1984). They also report on their own field study, which is the best of the four studies. Their research is more social science based than the other studies, which were conducted by security personnel. In each of these studies, random samples of customers were followed by trained observers as they shopped in the target store. Table 1.3 presents the findings of the four studies. The percentage of shoppers observed taking at least one item ranged from 0.8 percent to 8.4 percent in the eight stores. This suggests that certain characteristics of stores should also be considered as an important variable influencing the amount of shoplifting that occurs. Certain stores may be viewed as prime targets for shoplifting because of the nature or quality of merchandise, or because they are seen as having poor security. Another finding shown in Table 1.3 is that in half of the stores males were observed shoplifting more than females, and in the other half females were more likely to be observed shoplifting. It

Table 1.3
Observational Studies of Shoplifting

| | | % Shoplifting (N) | | |
Study	Description and Location of Shops	All	Men	Women
Astor	New York dept. store 1	8.4 (500)	6.4 (156)	9.2 (344)
(1971)	New York dept. store 2	5.2 (361)	5.7 (135)	5.3 (226)
	Boston dept. store	4.4 (404)	2.6 (149)	5.4 (255)
	Philadelphia dept. store	7.8 (382)	6.0 (132)	8.8 (250)
Group 4	U.K. dept. stores	0.8 (524)	1.9 (158)	0.3 (366)
(1972)	U.K. supermarkets	2.0 (494)	2.3 (131)	1.9 (363)
Marks	5 Dublin department	5.5 (567)	4.4 (180)	5.9 (387)
(1975)	and convenience stores			
Buckle	1 British dept. store	1.8 (503)	2.8 (142)	1.4 (361)
and				
Farrington				
(1984)				

Source: Adapted from Table 1 and Table 2 in Abigale Buckle and David P. Farrington (1984), "An Observational Study of Shoplifting" (*British Journal of Criminology* 24(1): 64, 68).

also appears that shoplifting occurs less frequently in England than in the United States or Ireland, but more data would be necessary to confirm this.

Another well-done observational study of a Chicago department store provides some additional insights (Baumer and Rosenbaum, 1984). This study added a new twist on how the percentage of shoplifters was calculated. In addition to the 2.7 percent of the 233 shoppers that the observers were "certain" had shoplifted, there was another 1.1 percent where it was "very probable" (e.g., the observer's view was shielded while an object in the person's hand disappeared) that shoplifting had occurred. Finally, confederate "shoplifters" were sent into the store to check on the accuracy of the observers. The observers detected "certain" and "very probable" shoplifting by only 45.9 percent of the confederate shoplifters. Rosenbaum and associates concluded that 7.8 percent of the observed shoppers had shoplifted. This percentage was based on what the observers had detected and was adjusted for the shoplifting that had occurred but had not been detected.

An interesting but more limited study trained observers to watch customer behavior in self-service bulk food sections of grocery stores

(Johnson et al., 1985). In 15 percent of the 867 interactions of a shopper with a food bin, the shopper tasted the product. This high percentage of technically legal "shoplifters" must be tempered with the realization that eating a couple of raisins or peanuts will rarely be treated as shoplifting by store personnel. When this practice, called grocery grazing (where customers eat or drink packaged and unpackaged products while shopping), results in the loss of more expensive items, then it is more likely to be viewed and treated as shoplifting. In conclusion, these observational statistics detected that from 1 percent to 15 percent of all shoppers in a store had shoplifted. This greatly increases the size of the shoplifting problem compared to that known to the police.

Likewise, self-report studies of shoplifting behavior have also found shoplifting to be much more frequent than is revealed in store apprehension studies. Lloyd Klemke's (1982a) study of high school students in four small communities revealed that 63 percent reported having shoplifted at some time in their lives.[5] A major study of a national sample of high school seniors showed that 39 percent of the males and 26.6 percent of the females admitted having shoplifted during the last year (Osgood et al., 1989). Several other self-report studies indicate that shoplifting was one of the top five types of delinquency committed by youth regardless of their sex or race (Gold, 1970; Hindelang et al., 1981).

One of the rare self-report surveys of adult shoplifting was conducted by Joann Ray (1987). She sought the cooperation of randomly selected shoppers at ten Spokane shopping centers. Unfortunately, only 38 percent of those asked, who said they would do so, returned their completed questionnaires. One out of twelve (8.9%) respondents admitted to shoplifting during the last year. In another project a questionnaire survey was sent to residents in southern California (Kallis and Vanier, 1985). Again there was a lack of cooperation, with only 27 percent returning a completed questionnaire. Eighteen percent of those responding admitted shoplifting during the last year.

Turning to a subculture of the population, there is good research documenting the reliance on shoplifting as an important source of funds for street heroin addicts (Inciardi, 1980; Johnson et al., 1985; Kowalski and Faupel, 1990). This evidence will be extensively developed in a later chapter.

In summary, a variety of research projects utilizing a wide range of different methods have been reviewed. There is consensus that shoplifting is a very frequent and costly type of deviance. Shoplifting is a significant component of the deviant repertoires of many youth, most delinquents, some adults, and certain deviant subcultures. Therefore, it should receive more research attention.

Finally, just as there are excellent reasons to seek general patterns and explanations of deviance and crime (Gottfredson and Hirschi, 1990), there is also merit in focusing on specific crimes (Meier, 1984). Several analysts have advocated this approach. Francis Cullen (1984), for example, has promoted the "structuring perspective," which is devoted to identifying the variables that explain why one type of deviance is selected and others are not. Similarly, Derek Cornish and Ronald Clarke (1986) focus on the criminal as a rational decision-maker. They feel it is important to conduct crime-specific analyses to discover the unique patterns underlying each type. For example, they point to research that has found differences between burglars and robbers and even subtle differences between commercial burglars and residential burglars. Cameron (1964) also raised this issue when she suggested that traditional explanations of deviance may not account for shoplifting done by "respectable" individuals. My analysis, while leaning toward the crime-specific approach, does not claim that this is the only or best strategy. Instead, it is claimed that both perspectives are needed. Therefore, shoplifting will be examined for how it is similar to and also how it is different from other types of deviance-crime.

OVERVIEW OF THE BOOK

The analysis will be divided in the following manner. Chapter 2 develops a qualitative look at shoplifting. Numerous historical and contemporary ethnographic accounts are presented to give a rich descriptive survey of the diverse manifestations of shoplifting. Chapter 3 focuses on quantitative research on shoplifting. In particular, I address the traditional "who shoplifts?" question. The focus is on identifying shoplifting patterns by age, sex, social class, and so forth. Store apprehension studies and self-report research are explored, reviewed, and critiqued. Chapter 4 explores various typologies that identify important distinctions for analyzing shoplifters and shoplifting behavior. Chapter 5 develops and analyzes the meaningfulness of the major psychiatric/ psychological and sociological theories of deviance-crime when applied to shoplifting. Qualitative and quantitative research evidence from the earlier chapters are woven into this analysis. The main sociological theories that are covered are anomie-strain, social control, differential association, neutralization, and rational choice theories. Chapter 6 examines research on how stores and the legal system deal with shoplifting and shoplifters. The deterrence and labeling theoretical perspectives are utilized to structure a review, critique, and analysis of the extensive literature. Various approaches to preventing and reducing shoplifting are also critically reviewed. Finally, a succinct final chapter provides an overview of the book.

NOTES

1. Sheriffs and police chiefs also consider shoplifting to be a low priority matter. In a national study of response priorities to 12 types of requests for police assistance, shoplifting was given priority only over responding to employee theft calls (Cunningham et al., 1990).

2. Many other types of deviant consumer behavior have been ignored by social scientists. See the questionnaire study of consumer attitudes toward 15 types of consumer fraud (e.g., returning an item that had been worn, not correcting a clerk who gives back too much change, or making out a check with insufficient funds) by Wilkes (1978) as a starting point for future research.

3. Several statements of the seriousness of the shoplifting problem from the retailer's perspective can be found in French et al. (1984) and *Business Week* (1979).

4. In fact, in *Uniform Crime Reports*, shoplifting known to the police has increased in almost every year since 1960, when the statistic was first reported.

5. A random sample of college students was surveyed by Kraut (1976). He reported that 61 percent of those returning the questionnaire admitted to having shoplifted at least once.

2

OF SHOPLIFTERS
AND SHOPLIFTING

The man's apartment, on the third floor of a yellow Victorian, resembled more than anything a warehouse, or a flea market. Hung from nails along the entryway was a wardrobe of cowboy hats with ornate, feathered hatbands, Greek fisherman's caps, felt fedoras. Rising from the far corner of the living-room floor like some unearthly shrubbery was a collection of fire extinguishers. Bordering that were stacks of brand-new hardcover books and a tower of cassette tapes, still in cellophane. A long, low table was crowded with digital clock-radios, Chinese porcelain, paperweights, empty picture frames. His one window was draped with a dozen glass crystals that quivered in the still air, disturbing the walls with prism colors. There was nothing casual about this man's shoplifting.

Ellen Lesser,
The Shoplifter's Apprentice (pp. 10–11)

While there is not a great deal of in-depth sociological research on shoplifting, many studies do refer to shoplifting in passing. This is especially the case for research projects on deviance that utilize an ethnographic, phenomenological, or case study methodology. It is not unusual to find references to shoplifters and shoplifting within the detailed descriptive accounts that have been obtained by these techniques. Usually, it is only a passing reference or a section of interview excerpts that illuminates the shoplifting facet of the research subject's deviant life-style.

This chapter accumulates a number of historical and contemporary examples that illustrate typical and atypical varieties of shoplifters and shoplifting. Obviously, these references do not constitute a representative sample of shoplifters. In fact, the examples are skewed toward cases where shoplifting has become, at least temporarily, a part of that person's life. Individuals who have shoplifted only a few times or on rare occasions are not emphasized here. Likewise, the examples are spread over a great span of time and are drawn from many research projects of varying degrees of quality. What these accounts may lack in terms of scientific rigor, however, is to some degree compensated for by their richness. Thus, these descriptive accounts provide a great deal of insight into the patterns of behavior and strategies, the social context, and sometimes the person's thinking and explanations for shoplifting behavior. The chapter pulls together this "soft" but rich material into a montage that will serve as a descriptive introduction to the phenomenon of shoplifters and shoplifting. While most of the accounts and excerpts are pregnant with sociological meaning, only minimal analysis is conducted in this chapter.

SHOPLIFTERS AND SHOPLIFTING FROM THE PAST

Shoplifting, like most types of deviance, has an extensive history. It was most likely a concern that plagued the first merchants who placed their goods out in a public market place. Cameron presents one of the earliest known accounts of a British professional shoplifting troupe operating in the year 1595. She quotes from Judges' study of the Elizabethan underworld.

The higher degree and gentlemen-lifts have to the performance of their faculty three parties of necessity, the lift, the marker, and the santar. The lift, attired in the form of a civil country gentlemen, comes with the marker into some mercer's shop, haberdasher's, goldsmith's or any such place where any particular parcels of worth are to be conveyed, and there he calls to see a bolt of satin, velvet, or any such commodity, and, not likeing the pile, colour, or brack, he calls for more, and whiles he begins to resolve which of them most fitly may be lifted, and what garbage (for so he calls the goods stolen) may be most easily conveyed. Then he calls to the mercer's man and says, "Sirrah, reach me that piece of velvet or satin, or that jewel, chain, or piece of plate"; and whilst the fellow turns his back, he commits his garbage to the marker; for note the lift is without his cloak, in his doublet and hose, to avoid the more suspicion: The marker, which is the receiver of the lift's luggage, gives a wink to the santar, that walks before the window, and then, the santar going by in great haste, the marker calls to him and says, "Sir, a word with you. I have a message to do unto you from a friend of yours, and the errand is of some importance."

"Truly sir," says the santar, "I have urgent business in hand, and as at this time I cannot stay."

"But one word, and no more," says the marker, and then he delivers to him whatsoever the lift has conveyed to him; and then the santar goes on his way, who never came within the shop, and is a man unknown to them all. (Judges, 1930: 170)

In the 1700s, shoplifters continued to plague shopkeepers even though they could be sent to the gallows if they were caught. In 1726 shop-keepers desiring even more help requested that the government assist them by offering a reward and a pardon for anyone who would inform on their fellow shoplifters. A so-called "woman Burton" responded to this offer and informed on her associates Jane Holmes and Mary Robin-son and their fence, Jonathan Wild. The three were apprehended, tried, and executed for their crimes (Cameron, 1964).

Henry Mayhew crafted detailed descriptive documents about the lives of the residents of London during the mid–1800s. He pioneered in study-ing the lives of the poor and not-so-poor criminal elements of this great city. At one point, he focused on shoplifters. His lengthy and instructive summary is presented as follows:

There is a class of women who visit the shops in various parts of the metropolis, sometimes two and at other times three together. They vary their dress according to the locality they visit. Sometimes you find them dressed very respectably, like the wives of people in good circumstances in life; at other times, they appear like servants. They often wear large cloaks, or shawls, and are to be found of different ages, from 14 to 60. They generally call into shops at busy times, when there are many persons standing around the counter, and will stand two or three together. They ask a look of certain articles, and will possibly say, after they have inspected them, that they do not suit them; they will say they are too high in price, or not the article they want, or not the proper colour. They will likely ask to see some other goods, and keep looking at the different articles until they get a quantity on the counter. When the shopman is engaged getting some fresh goods from the window, or from the shelves, one of them generally contrives to slip something under her cloak or shawl, while the other manages to keep his attention abstracted. Sometimes they carry a bag or a basket, and set it down on the counter, and while the shopman is busy, they will get some article and lay it down behind their basket, such as a roll of ribbons, or a half dozen of gloves, or other small portable goods. While the shopman's back is turned, or his attention withdrawn, it is hidden under their shawl or cloak. We frequently find the skirt of their dress lined from the pocket downward, forming a large repository all around the dress, with an opening in front, where they can insert a small articles, which is not observed in the ample crinoline. In stealing rolls of silk, or other heavier goods, they conceal them under their arm. Women who engage in shoplifting sometimes pick pockets in the shops. They get by the side of a lady engaged looking over articles, and under pretense of inspecting goods in the one hand, pick their pockets with the other.

We find more of these people living in the east end and on the Surrey side than in the west end of the metropolis. A great many live in the neighbourhood of

Kingsland Road and Hackney Road. Some of them cohabit with burglars, others with magsmen (skittle-sharps).

We find ladies in respectable position occasionally charged with shoplifting.

Respectably dressed men frequently go into the shops of drapers and others early in the morning, or at intervals during the day, or evening, to look at the goods, and often manage to abstract one or two articles, and secrete them under their coats. They frequently take a bundle of neckties, a parcel of gloves, or anything that will go in a small compass, and perhaps enter a jeweller's shop, and in this way abstract a quantity of jewellery. On going there, they will ask a sight of some articles; the first will not suit them, and they will ask to look at more. When the shopman is engaged, they will abstract some gold rings or gold pins, or other property, sometimes a watch. Occasionally they will go so far as to leave a deposit on the article, promising to call again. They do this to prevent suspicion. After they are gone, the shopman may find several valuables missing.

Sometimes they will ring the changes. On entering the shop they will bring patterns of rings and other articles in the window, which they have got made as facsimiles from metal of an inferior quality. On looking at the jewellery they will ring the changes on the counter, and keep turning them over, and in so doing abstract the genuine article and leave the counterfeit in its place. (Mayhew, 1968: 311)

Herbert Asbury (1927) provided a similar chronicle of life in the notorious Five Points slum area of New York City during the 1800s and early 1900s. He noted that shoplifting was one of the forms of crime and vice that was rampant in this area. Youth were mentioned more prominently than in Mayhew's London. Gangs of young males, such as the Forty Little Thieves, Little Dead Rabbits, and the most famous, the Whyos, are made up of thugs, thieves, and murderers. These gangs were extensively involved in endless variations of theft, such as till-tapping, picking pockets, burglary, and the ubiquitous shoplifting. He also reported on bands of homeless boys and girls being led by an adult who taught them the many forms of thievery. Sometimes the shoplifting bordered on robbery, as when a dozen thugs would ride up to a butcher shop, rush inside, and seize a carcass of beef, hams, and as much of other cuts of meat as they could carry. They would then rush out and flee the area.

Adults were also identified by Asbury as being involved in shoplifting pursuits. He described how middle-aged Black Lena, who had been successfully involved in thievery and blackmail, settled into a routine of shoplifting and pickpocket activity. She posed as the wealthy widow of a mining engineer living in Hackensack, New Jersey. After hosting many elaborate social functions she attained the reputation of the Queen of Hackensack. Her ability to maintain this extravagant life-style was dependent upon her frequent shoplifting and pickpocketing forays into New York City.

Between 1870 and the early 1900s much attention was given to an "epidemic" of shoplifting. As almost every era has seen similar claims, one might be skeptical of these assertions. There is, however, consensus that a new and puzzling dimension had been added to the phenomenon of shoplifting. For the first time, significant numbers of *middle-class* females were being apprehended for shoplifting. While stores were reluctant to publicize this trend, it soon became a favorite topic for newspaper and magazine articles. It also was the subject for stage plays, silent movies (e.g., "Kleptomania" and "The Kleptomaniac"), and songs ("Mamie, Don't You Feel Ashamie") (Abelson, 1989b: 216). Fortunately, there are several recent historical works that carefully and insightfully analyze *what* was happening and, perhaps more importantly, how this trend was *interpreted* by the decision-makers of that era (Abelson, 1989b: O'Brien, 1983).

Elaine Abelson's thorough and excellent historical analysis focused mainly on New York City. Patricia O'Brien concentrated on France, where over 200 case studies of bourgeois female shoplifters had been published. Both of these writers document the emergence and popularization of the medical diagnosis of kleptomania to account for the "irrational actions" of "light-fingered ladies." How else could one explain the behavior of a lady who, while "stealing an umbrella worth 3 francs 95 centimes, had 70,000 francs in her purse at the time of the theft" (O'Brien, 1983: 67)? Medical specialists were initially called in to diagnose these types of cases and found numerous variations of "sexual physiological accidents and problems" such as menopause, regular and irregular menstruation, pregnancy, and unfulfilled sexual desires. One shoplifter even confided that she "got more pleasure from her thefts than from the father of her children" (O'Brien, 1983: 68).

Psychiatrists soon came into the picture and redefined the cause of these types of shoplifting as pathological *mental* conditions instead of pathological *physical* conditions. Both Abelson and O'Brien agree that because this new breed of shoplifters came from affluent families, new explanations were created to minimize the guilt of these ladies. Stores, for example, did not want to antagonize their affluent clientele. Families who wanted to keep their moral reputations untarnished sought the counsel of medical and psychiatric "experts." Even the courts did not want to convict "respectable ladies" as common criminals. Therefore, the diagnosis of kleptomania was socially constructed by key decision-makers to deal with these sensitive cases, thus "legitimatizing" the actions of the stores and courts to dismiss or acquit those afflicted with this "women's sickness."

Abelson and O'Brien agree that a major factor underlying the overall increase in shoplifting, and that by bourgeois ladies, was the emergence of the department store. Abelson in particular elaborates on the role that these new shopping meccas played in hastening the transformation of females from *producers* of family clothes and the like, in their own homes, into customers who *shopped* to meet their families needs. A consumption culture was fostered by new mass retailing practices and advertising.[1] Department stores were designed to heighten sensory stimulation and create a desire for the merchandise. Show windows displayed the latest fashions to lure people into the store. Mirrors, lights, and a profusion of goods that one could touch were attractively displayed. Stores sponsored many sales and special events to attract large crowds and generate enthusiasm for their merchandise. The downside of this often successful orchestration to create a desire for merchandise was that some customers did not pay for all of the items that they took out of the stores. According to the view, popular at that time, this new level of temptation and the assignment of shopping to weak-willed and sexually disordered females inevitably led to more shoplifting.

In the 1920s and 1930s sociologists at the University of Chicago began to put their unique stamp on the sociology of deviance-crime. The so-called Chicago School of sociologists exhorted researchers to go out into society and study people in their social worlds. This led to many interesting studies of hobos, taxi dancers, youth gangs, and criminals. Frederick Thrasher's (1927) classic study, *The Gang*, described stealing as the leading predatory activity of the adolescent gang. Included among these youths' endless variations of theft (e.g., burglary, picking pockets, jack rolling, etc.) was a heavy reliance on shoplifting. Thrasher presents a detailed description of one gang that illustrates the pervasiveness of shoplifting as a major component of its stealing repertoire:

The Black Hand Society is a gang of about fifteen boys, twelve to fifteen years old, all of whom are Jewish with the exception of two Italians. . . . Clownie, the first leader of the Black Handers, was a half-wit, but he was an expert little thief, and it is he who introduced the "art" of stealing and organized the boys in this neighborhood into the Black Hand gang. Quicker than lightning, he made his way in and out among the crowded groups of Maxwell Street market place, stealing first this and then that. He had money; indeed everything he wanted. And there was excitement, too. Sometimes he would almost get caught; but always, just as the women in their stalls began to wrangle with him and to lose their heads in their anger, he would vanish. That was fun, devilish good sport. . . . Stealing offers to the members of the gang about the easiest way of getting the means to satisfy their wishes. Itschkie was told that he and his gang ought to clean up a bit. He agreed. The next day or so saw more than one of his pals cleaned up, dressed in new clothes, and all the rest of it. Itschkie appeared himself in a completely new outfit. One can have little doubt as to where the money came from, for a similar thing happened only recently, shortly after the group was known to have made a raid upon one of the stores.

The stealing of candy, fruits, cameras, and similar luxuries is of course, too commonplace to deserve special mention, for there is hardly a time when the group goes out on a spree that it does not indulge its desires in this manner. (Thrasher, 1927: 215–18).

Clifford Shaw and Henry D. McKay, key figures of the Chicago School, promoted the life-history (also referred to as the case study or auto-biography) research technique. They felt it was very important to obtain extensive detailed descriptions of the criminal's "own story" in order "to understand and correct an offender" (Snodgrass, 1982: 4). Shaw generated several monographs that have become classic documents il-lustrating this qualitative research strategy. In *The Natural History of a Delinquent*, Clifford Shaw (1931) presents Sidney's story of his progres-sion in delinquency up to his arrest at age 16 for robbery and rape. Eight of Sidney's 21 legal entanglements were for shoplifting. The shoplifting arrests were accumulated between his seventh and eleventh birthdays. Sidney describes his introduction and involvement in shoplifting as follows:

Shortly after this I became acquainted with a boy named Joseph Kratz who lived a few doors from where I lived. Joseph was about four years older than I was and knew quite a lot. He knew so much about life and I liked him, so I made him my idol. At first he would not allow me to go places with him because I was so much younger than he was. But finally he allowed me to accompany him after school and we became fast friends. He proved to be very fast indeed; for one day while we were passing a fruit store he picked up an apple while no one was looking and continued to walk past the store with the apple in his hand. He performed for me in like manner quite a few times and nothing would do but that he must teach me to do the same thing. That was the first time I ever stole anything. . . . The proprietor soon discovered what was going on and in his endeavor to curtail further depredations on his stock began to keep a sharp lookout for our approach and to watch closely as we passed. This only made the game more interesting and it began to require real skill to get away with anything. Often after this he would chase us for a block or two in order to teach us a lesson but he never did. This is when it started to get real good and you couldn't keep us away after that. The chases added spice to our little game. (Shaw, 1931: 57–58)

New adventures and temptations arose as they discovered the fairy-land variety of stores in the Loop of downtown Chicago. Joseph again led the way:

Joseph knew just what to do to make money unnecessary. He taught me to shoplift and most of the little things that we stole were useless. We'd steal from one counter and wander to another part of the floor and steal from another counter. We'd go to another floor and do the same thing over. I thought we were too slick for anybody to catch us. . . . Then store detectives started following us; but we didn't worry about them. It seemed we always saw them first and it was a simple matter to dodge through the store and lose them. Joseph often told me to keep my mouth shut if we ever got caught and to beg for a chance. Two or three times a store detective caught us in the act of filching an article and because I cried we were turned loose. The first time that I was arrested, I was handled as an adult criminal would have been. . . . No sooner was I taken to one of the store's private offices, than a call was put in for the police. . . . At the C——Police Station I was handled as perfunctorily as at the department store. I was only about seven and a half years old and being half scared to death at the prospect of being locked into a cell. (Shaw, 1931: 66–67)

Spending many hours in a jail cell had little impact on this youngster. Instead he "grew more wary and kept a keen watch for house detectives and made more of an effort to get away from them when about to be apprehended" (Shaw, 1931: 68). Even so he accumulated at least seven more arrests for shoplifting, indicating as he says, "stealing. It was my daily occupation and fast becoming a part of my life" (Shaw, 1931: 68).

In *The Jack-Roller*, Shaw (1930) presents Stanley's story. His delinquent and criminal involvements resulted in 38 arrests. His early arrests were primarily for running away from home and truancy. There was a considerable amount of involvement with theft and specifically shoplifting, but he was only arrested several times for shoplifting. Stanley's step-brother, his brother's friends, and his sisters were all active in shoplifting and encouraged the younger Stanley to emulate their behavior. His despised step-mother actually sent him out, with her other children, to shoplift items she needed. After numerous corrupting incarceration experiences, Stanley became more involved in jack-rolling drunks.

CONTEMPORARY SHOPLIFTERS AND SHOPLIFTING

The colorful historical review that we have just completed indicates that shoplifting has long been a popular type of deviance. This picturesque tradition continues unabated into the contemporary era. Even though modern retailing and advertising have become more sophisticated and security personnel and technology have been upgraded, shoplifting has retained much of its historical form. Recent research identifies various segments of the population that exhibit high levels of involvement in shoplifting. Several of these special types of shoplifters are illustrated in the following examples drawn from contemporary sources.

Youth, for example, continue to exhibit high levels of shoplifting activity. One example, from a middle-class setting, is provided by researcher Norman Weiner, who posed as a high school student. During his participant observation study he recorded this account of a "shopping" trip with Karen, a dentist's daughter. At one of the stores Karen bought a blouse and tried on several dresses. Before leaving the store, they stopped at a cosmetics counter, where he saw her put some mascara into her purse with a grin. After they had left the store he asked her why she had done that. She said:

"Didn't you take anything?"
I shrugged noncommitally, "No, really. Why'd you take it?"
"I needed it."
"But you could have paid for it. I'd have paid for it if you wanted it that badly."
"This is easier."
As we walked back to the car, she continued to talk. "Well, you know, I don't do it all the time. And I only get what I really need. Like that mascara. But not what I don't need, 'cause that's dumb. Nobody misses stuff in a store like that. I mean, everyone does it. It's easy to get things. Even like this dress."
"What dress?"
"Huh?" She seemed surprised I hadn't known. She opened the bag she had been holding, and there, along with the blouse she had paid for, was a dress.
"But the bag was stapled."
"I put it in the bag in the dressing room. With this." She opened her purse and showed me a stapler with a staple remover. (Weiner, 1970: 216)

Weiner comments, "Karen is not unusual, her whole crowd steals. The same reasons are always heard: 'I needed it; I only take from big stores.' They never use the word 'steal.' It is always 'get' " (1970: 216).

An upper-class respondent shared the following account with me of her active shoplifting involvement while in high school.

When did you get involved in taking things from stores?

Mostly in high school, those were the big days. We'd go on shoplifting sprees, we'd have a contest. There were seven or eight of us and we'd have a time period say three hours, usually from lunch to the end of school. And whoever could shoplift the most stuff and bring it all back to an agreed upon spot, and the one who got the most stuff and most expensive stuff won.

What were the other kids like?

It was the doper crowd, mostly guys from an affluent suburb.

What precautions did you take?

We were good, we didn't care if we were caught. We weren't scared, I know I would just walk in and pick something up and walk out. I wouldn't hide it or anything. Like one time I got this imitation fur coat. I had a sweater on, it was really cold outside and everyone was wearing coats anyway, so I just put the coat on and tucked the tags up the sleeve and casually walked out. It was outrageous, it was fun!

How much would you steal during a shoplifting competition?

One day we met we had over $700.00 of stuff between the 6–7 of us. One guy had a portable TV and a bunch of other good stuff. He won all of it, but he'd give us what we wanted. The hardest part was telling our parents where we got it from. I told my mom that Mary's mom, who's immensely rich, bought it for us.

Another adolescent respondent, the daughter of a public school principal, described an ironical set of circumstances that led to her involvement in shoplifting. While the family was financially secure, her parents did not provide her with enough financial support to keep her in minimal school supplies or suitably clothed. This led to her resorting to shoplifting, always in a neighboring community, for these essentials. She was also experiencing problems with her family relationships. She was close to her father, but he was always at meetings and school functions. Therefore she felt neglected by him. Her mother was preoccupied with her own problems and had become engrossed in pursuing a college degree. The mother expected the girl to "be her servant" and do all the household chores and prepare the meals. Once, when the daughter had forgotten to take meat out of the freezer for dinner, the mother became irate. During this confrontation the mother 'threw the package of frozen meat and hit me in the leg because she was so mad." This girl felt that the economic pressure and the unhappy home situation contributed to her brief, but active, high school career in shoplifting. Her eventual apprehension for shoplifting brought her involvement to a traumatic conclusion.

Likewise, adult middle-class female shoplifters continue to be a significant segment of the contemporary shoplifting population. Besides Cameron's original analysis of "respectable" shoplifters, however, very few systematic studies are available to verify that these types of females are over-represented in the ranks of shoplifters. Even so, many commentators have made this claim (e.g., Kopecky, 1980; Brenton, 1985; Bernikow, 1988; Pousner, 1988). While it is still an open question as to the exact extent of their contribution to shoplifting statistics, there is ample evidence that a surprising number of women do shoplift. The following excerpts, drawn from journalistic sources, provide instructive examples of adult female shoplifters.

Michael Pousner, illustrating what he calls a "yuppie female crime," describes Jane, an extreme example of this type, as follows:

Jane has a high paying job as an executive for a prestigious Atlanta advertising agency. She also has a new maroon BMW and a closet full of Ralph Lauren and other designer clothes she has shoplifted from good Atlanta stores. "It's incredibly easy to steal from a retail store," says Jane, "and once you succeed it's hard to stop." Jane's thefts—of tens, if not hundreds, of thousands of dollars in merchandise over the years—invariably gave her a kick. "My most successful night was when I walked away with a raccoon coat and three Calvin Klein suits." (Pousner, 1988: 167)

Similarly, Louise Bernikow points to the importance of how a woman looks. In the past this was linked to being attractive for dating and marriage; today there is also the necessity of looking good in order to be upwardly mobile. She illustrates this with Carol, an expensive clothes shoplifter, who wants to move up the corporate ladder.

"At my office it is very important to look rich, to look successful. It doesn't matter whether you are or not, just that you look a certain way. I share an apartment with two other girls and I almost never eat dinner in restaurants. All my money goes for clothes." Carol works in the financial district in New York City. She reads all the upscale fashion magazines. And she falls into fits of envy and despair. "I'd have to pool my income with my roommates," she says, "and maybe together the three of us could afford to buy *one* of these suits." (Bernikow, 1988: 281)

Myron Brenton (1985) claims that more adult female shoplifters are like Janet, who has a good management position but is also a confirmed shoplifter. Every couple of weeks she mixes with the hordes of shoppers and deftly drops into her shoulder bag a tube of lipstick or some costume jewelry. The author suggests that she does this in response to dissatisfaction in the most intimate areas of her life: love, sex, and family relationships.

Finally, just like the underworld of Mayhew's London or Asbury's New York, shoplifting still appears to be a regular part of the cultural landscape of contemporary slum communities. This is especially the case for the subculture of street-level heroin abusers (Hanson et al., 1985; Jarvis and Parker, 1989). The most extensive research project to target this subculture is *Taking Care of Business* (Johnson et al., 1985). This field study obtained in-depth material on the economics of crime from a sample of 201 New York City drug addicts. Thumbnail sketches of two subjects are presented in the following vignette:

W. J. (black male, age 37) was a daily heroin user who specialized in boosting (shoplifting) from stores; he would then retail fence (sell) the items to people in the street, bars, or other neighborhood locations. He was interviewed for thirty-three days and reported shoplifting on 18 percent of those days. He earned anywhere from $20 to $150 per incident, averaging $36. On an annual basis, he would have committed 376 such offenses, earning $13,483. Some examples follow:

11/12/81   Stole a coat, two pairs of shoes, and cosmetics from four stores; got $100 for the goods.

11/13/81   Stole five pairs of adult jeans (worth $25 to $30 each), six pairs of children's jeans (worth $12 to $13)), eight ski masks, two shirts, a belt, and some socks. Kept the belt, sold all the other items for a total of $114.

11/14/81   Stole two coats from a department store; got $150 for them.

11/16/81   Stole a coat and a pair of jeans from two stores; sold the items to two persons and made $80.

Klip N. (black male, age 30) used heroin daily, was a low-level thief who specialized in cattle rustling (stealing meat from grocery stores) and selling it to neighborhood people, who bought whenever it was available. He was interviewed for thirty-three days and reported shoplifting on twenty-eight of those days. He committed forty-two shoplifting offenses, twenty-seven (68 percent) of which involved stealing and reselling meat; Klip got an average of $15 per theft. (Johnson et al., 1985: 51)

Another individual with a long drug and criminal history is found in the excellent case study *Manny: A Criminal-Addict's Story* (Rettig et al., 1977). Growing up in New York City in the 1950s, Manny was exposed to and became involved in many underworld scenes such as gangs, drugs, and rackets. At one time he became quite successful in an illicit check-cashing scheme and at another time in a gambling organization. Addiction to heroin, however, distracted him from stable sources of illicit success and he resorted to quick money schemes to get drug money. He describes one of his boosting routines:

But boosting is something different. I started out in markets and drug stores boosting cigarettes. Me and this kid worked as a team. We'd find a store, usually uptown, that didn't cover their cigarettes but left them out in open racks. One of us would stand point while the other would go under the coat or shirt with three or four cartons of butts.

Like, it's easy. You get a grocery cart and put a few items in it. You have an old envelope or something in your hand like a grocery list from the old lady. This is your front. You act like a legitimate shopper in the eyes of people around you. When you learn how to arrange your clothes right, you can get maybe four or five cartons underneath your belt. Each carton was worth a buck then, and usually the connection would take them for dope. So you boost cigarettes and get down. (Rettig et al., 1977: 40)

He also describes going into Macy's, picking out the biggest TV, brazenly getting a clerk to get him a dolly, and wheeling it out of the store. His most sophisticated boosting occurred when he connected with an experienced fur booster who recruited him to be her front man. She schooled him on the technique, outfitted him with a fine wardrobe, and then ran him through a trial run. When this went smoothly they graduated to the real thing.

First, the morning of the hit we go down and rent a Lincoln Continental. Like, it cost us about thirty bucks for two hours. And we drive down to where the fur warehouses are. We drive right up to the door of one of the fine shops, and someone comes out to the car to help us. Fran would start out talking about what kind of a fur she wanted. Man that broad had class. She really knew her furs! She would run it down to them about how she had to have a certain cut and just the proper grade of fur. That kind of stuff I never could figure out. I didn't understand what they were talking about.

So Fran would go off with the saleslady, who by now was conned into "knowing" she had a sure sale. And I would just start talking a blue streak to whoever it was—the manager or one of the salesladies. And tell them that I didn't know anything about the fur business or the product. "But my wife here wants to buy a coat, and she knows about it, so you know, I just hope that we don't get taken. Cause whatever she decides on I'm gonna have to buy it for her. I promised her for two years that I'm gonna do something big for her, and this is sort of a present." I'd just keep on talking like I don't know much. I'm a poor slob who happens to have a little bit of money. And the wife is spending it all up, y'know, running around from shop to shop. This is all part of the scam. And I just keep on running it down to them. I just rap on and keep telling them stuff like, "My poor wife can never make up her mind. This is the third time we've been down here. We keep going in these places and she keeps walking out on me. You know, leaves me stranded half the time. I'm liable to look up and that crazy broad'll be over in the shop next door or someplace." This effectively sets up in his mind that me and her may not necessarily leave together. That when I leave my wife might not be with me because she might have just walked out. So, I just keep on rapping like that, usually for ten or fifteen minutes. . . . So when Fran found the right coat (often she had an order from our main fence, Mickey, or some other fence) she would just walk out. If problems developed because the store personnel was hanging too close to her or the door, I would create a diversion by asking about a coat or some product in the back of the store.

After Fran split with the fur piece, I would just keep walking around acting as if I was intensely interested in the furs until I heard someone say something like, "The last time I saw her she was over here."

And I'd say, "Aw, shit, she must have left me again," and I'd do the irate husband trip and act like I was very fed up. (Rettig et al., 1977: 48–49)

After three months this successful liaison terminated and Manny reverted back to the street drug scene. Hitting bottom, he again resorted to shoplifting out of necessity. This incident unexpectedly transformed him into a career robber, as he describes:

I was hungry one day, really hungry. I hadn't had much of anything to eat for days. And, I went into this little grocery store to steal something to eat. But I was so sick and spaced out that I couldn't even take care of business, and this clerk caught me in the act. He made a grab for me to try and hold me until the cops could come, but I got my gun out and threw down on him. Now I was committed. You know what I mean? They just froze, and I said, "All right, just stand there while I just take what I need." So I took it. I walked the clerk around and had him fill up a shopping bag full of cigarettes, candy, and stuff to eat. I got the money out of the till, made both clerks empty their pockets, and even looked under the counter to see if they had any large bills stashed. I made the clerks go back in the walk-in freezer. Then I took out of there fast. I got me a hotel room not far away. I washed up, ate, scored some dope, and relaxed. I said, Okay, Manny, this is it. I'm going to steal what I need, take what I want, and to hell with it from now on.

Right there my life changed dramatically. I met up with four or five guys that were heavy into robbery on almost a daily basis. (Rettig et al., 1977: 57)

ATYPICAL SHOPLIFTERS

The previous examples illustrate common types of shoplifters. They reveal a broad spectrum of poor and affluent, male and female, juvenile and adult, and amateur and more "professionalized" shoplifters. This diversity can be underscored even further by highlighting some of the more atypical manifestations of shoplifting. For example, the popular stereotypes of the psychologically disturbed shoplifter and the elderly shoplifter, have probably received more attention (recall the earlier discussion on kleptomania) than their numbers would justify. Severe mental and emotional problems were identified as being evident in only 1.7 percent of the 300 convicted shoplifters interviewed by Richard Moore (1984). Three illustrative examples of what he called episodic shoplifters are summarized as follows:

A pattern of stealing laxatives was present for about seven years. The person steals a bottle of laxative, drinks the entire bottle in a short time, and suffers severe diarrhea for several hours. The episodes were triggered by contact with the person's mother.

During a period of about two and one-half years, the person stole food, consumed large quantities until vomiting occurred, and suffered for several hours. The episodes occurred whenever the person encountered disappointment perceived as failure in achieving vocational goals.

A pattern of stealing cosmetics was present for about one and one-half years. The stolen cosmetics were placed on a table at home, then the person would berate herself for stealing. Verbal abuse often continued for several hours, including screaming, sobbing, and crying. The episodes were triggered when a man expressed interest in developing a close heterosexual relationship. (Moore, 1984: 57)

While there are several statistical studies of elderly shoplifters, there is little systematic interview research. In a journalistic treatment of the topic titled "When Grandma Is a Thief," Marvin Grosswirth (1981) presents several explanations obtained from detained elderly shoplifters. Their responses ranged from "I'm tired of eating dog food and I felt like eating a decent piece of meat" to the other extreme, that "Society owes it to me. I'm just taking back what is rightfully mine" (Grosswirth, 1981: 75)

Additional illustrations of the diversity within the phenomenon of shoplifting are shown in the following examples. During the tumultuous 1960s era, activist Jerry Rubin (1970) proclaimed that shoplifting was a legitimate act against the capitalist establishment. Similarly, Abbie Hoffman (1971) advocated shoplifting as a political act in his notorious and controversial publication, *Steal This Book.*[2] Countering these examples with a touch of irony, Gary Marx (1988) discovered six cases of undercover cops being apprehended for shoplifting. While not seriously studying this anomalous behavior, he does speculate that undercover agents may "become" the seamy characters that they are posing as, and also that undercover agents may take advantage of their situation because they feel that they are immune from prosecution.

Other atypical shoplifters include prominent politicians, religious leaders, royalty, actresses, beauty queens, and other affluent public figures (Murphy, 1986; Dowling, 1988; *Jet*, 1989; *Time*, 1986; Bernikow, 1988). Several examples illustrate these types of shoplifters. James Wentzel, chief of Legal Services Corporation (a presidentially appointed position) was arrested for taking $5.66 worth of items from a supermarket (*U.S. News & World Report*, December 1, 1986). More recently, former glamour queen Hedy Lamarr was arrested for shoplifting $21 in "personal care items" from a drug store (*The Register-Guard*, 1991). The prestigious social positions and the absence of dire financial need make these cases of shoplifting puzzling and presumably rare.

SHOPLIFTING TECHNIQUES AND STRATEGIES

While many historical and contemporary examples of shoplifting have been presented, it is still instructive to look more closely at the range of techniques utilized by various shoplifters. Cameron (1964) devotes a chapter to the "Arts and Crafts" of shoplifting. It is also a favorite topic of security-oriented works seeking to alert others to the deceptive tactics used by shoplifters (e.g., Edwards, 1970; Baumer and Rosenbaum, 1984; Purpura, 1984). Only a representative sample of the almost endless tactics is outlined here. Two primary methods can be utilized. Some shoplifters choose to conceal the item(s), while others do not. Most shoplifters use the first tactics and hide the item(s) in pockets, purses, under their clothing, in other products, and so forth. Shoplifters may dress in bulky clothing, or those who specialize as "thigh boosters" may wear long skirts to hide items carried between their legs. Others carry aids and props into the store to assist their thefts. Security personnel are always alert to customers entering the store with a bag obtained from a prior visit (often called a bad bag) that may be used to stash items. One of my respondents utilized a large shopping bag that she had affectionately named her "klepto bag." There are examples of individuals who have faked broken arms or pregnancies to provide a hiding place for merchandise. A few employ the use of a "booster box," which appears to be a wrapped package but has a disguised opening to insert the item being taken (throughout the book I have inserted instructive shoplifting insights into "Booster Boxes"). These "professionalized props" may reduce chances of being apprehended but may complicate the situation if one is caught because one can hardly feign being a novice shoplifter.

Other shoplifters use more brazen tactics whereby they do not conceal the item being taken. One of my respondents described her technique as follows:

I would just walk in and pick something up and walk out. I wouldn't hide it or anything. Like one time I got this imitation fur coat. I had a sweater on, it was really cold outside and everyone was wearing coats anyway, so I just put the coat on and tucked the tags up the sleeve and casually walked out. It was outrageous, it was fun!

Many shoplifters feel that by employing this blatant tactic they will be more risk-free than someone who "sneaks around and cautiously awaits the opportune moment to take something." Another bold variation is to take an item and, without leaving the store, attempt to obtain a cash refund by claiming one is returning an item received as a gift. Some forgo fabricating any pretense at all; they simply grab an armful of valuable merchandise and depend on foot speed to make their getaway.

As we have seen in earlier examples, some shoplifters prefer to operate by themselves, whereas others (like Manny) team up with others to carry out their thefts. The advantages and benefits of having a supporting cast will be developed in Chapter 5. Finally, most shoplifters operate without the benefit of having a colleague employed by the store being targeted. On the other hand, it constitutes a tremendous advantage if one does have a friend or relative "inside" who will obligingly look the other way or ring up only the cheap items that one takes out of the store. Sometimes the insider may not even know that he or she is being used by the resourceful thief. For example, a seemingly respectable customer coming out of the store may flash a receipt at a naive box boy who is just returning to the store. The customer who is carrying a bag of groceries may request that the box boy please load several bags of dog food or fertilizer into the trunk and thank the youngster for the assistance. A security respondent reported that he once observed several hundred dollars worth of merchandise being shoplifted in this manner. These examples illustrate some of the tactics and strategies used by clever and imaginative shoplifters.

CONCLUSIONS

The intent of this chapter has been to expose the reader to the tremendous diversity of people and types of behavior involved in shoplifting. This complexity poses a formidable challenge to the student of shoplifting who is attempting to make sense of this behavior. The accounts presented here are in no way intended to be representative of the population of shoplifters. They have, however, been selected because they do illustrate patterns found in a variety of sources. The examples are particularly biased in portraying more adults and more individuals who are repeatedly or "professionally" involved with shoplifting than would probably be found in a representative sample of shoplifters.

Even though the material in this chapter was not intended to be subjected to rigorous analysis, some very broad tentative generalizations seem to be warranted. The shoplifters described in this chapter are (1) coming from all age groups, particularly youth through middle age; (2) continuing a pattern of shoplifting that sometimes started in their childhood; (3) sometimes springboarding from shoplifting to other types of deviance and vice versa, or are regularly involved in a variety of other types of deviant acts; (4) taking items for personal use and/or as a significant mode of fulfilling their own economic needs; (5) likely to be with others at the time of the offense (this is particularly the case for youth and for adults who were "professional" shoplifters); (6) more likely to be females than would be the case for most other types of crimes; (7) sometimes experiencing a variety of economic, personal, and interpersonal difficulties in their lives; (8) commenting on how "easy" it is to do; and (9) utilizing a variety of techniques and strategies, many of which have been used for centuries.

The next three chapters refine and elaborate this analysis of shoplifting. Chapter 3 considers the variety of statistical studies of shoplifting. In particular, quantitative studies of individuals apprehended for shoplifting and self-report studies are reviewed and analyzed. Chapter 4 looks at a variety of typologies of shoplifting and shoplifters. Chapter 5 explores the meaningfulness of psychological and sociological theories of deviance to help understand shoplifting behavior.

NOTES

1. Another excellent historical analysis of this era and particularly the role of advertising is developed by Stuart Ewen in *Captains of Consciousness: Advertising and the Social Roots of the Consumer Culture* (1976).

2. Original copies of *Steal This Book* have become collectors' items. For obvious reasons, libraries have been unable to keep copies on their shelves. It is also interesting to note that the sections describing shoplifting techniques have been used to train new security personnel on what they should be looking for.

3

FACES IN THE CROWD:
WHO SHOPLIFTS?

Charles M. Lewis Jr. has an office at the new Lionel Kiddie City Toys store on 34th Street in Manhattan that looks like a control room of any television network. Six TV monitors, each wired to as many as four cameras, allow Lionel's metro manager to track customers from the front entrance until they exit. The complex television system is a security measure, of course. Mug shots of recent shoplifters, pinned to a nearby wall, are evidence of that.

Chain Store Age Executive, 1989 (p. 36)

Who does it? Who are the shoplifters among us as we browse, shop, and people-watch at our favorite malls and stores? This chapter initiates the search for the types of people who are more active in shoplifting. Perhaps some clarification is necessary because of the chapter title. A revival of Caesar Lombroso's (Lombroso and Ferrero, 1898) search for an identifiable face or body type that would allow security personnel to zero in on likely shoplifters is *not* what this chapter is about. Interestingly, many security personnel whom I have talked to believe that they *can* detect prospective shoplifters. Usually, they indicate that they are alerted more by how the person *acts* (i.e., a customer who is constantly looking at other people rather than at the merchandise) than by how the person *looks*. Daniel Murphy (1986) reports similar findings. Because there is not an identifiable shoplifters' face or body type, the analysis will instead focus on traditional demographic variables such as gender, age, social class, and subcultural involvements.

As in many other areas of deviance and crime, answering even simple questions—such as which sex or age group is more active in shoplifting—

is more difficult than one would expect. This chapter reviews the quantitative research devoted to identifying the types of people who shoplift. The studies utilize a variety of sociological research methodologies. There are, for example, studies based on store apprehension or police records, others that utilize self-report data, and some that rely on field observations. Each of these strategies offers a unique but limited perspective on shoplifting. Evaluating projects with different methodologies allows a more balanced assessment of who shoplifts.

EARLY-ERA SHOPLIFTING RESEARCH

The early era of studies on shoplifting, 1963 to 1971, concentrated on store apprehension data. This follows a historical trend in that most of the initial crime and delinquency research was based on "official statistics." In this case, the early shoplifting studies utilized store records instead of police records. This was expedient because store records were fairly accessible to researchers. They also provided a better sample than police records, because many of the individuals apprehended by stores are not passed on to the police.

The most significant early study of store records was Cameron's *The Booster and the Snitch* (1964). She analyzed data from a large sample of individuals apprehended in a major Chicago department store that she called Lakeside Co. Her work constitutes the most important sociological monograph devoted to shoplifting. Therefore, it has become a benchmark study serving as a stimulus and a point of comparison for subsequent research. Because the study has been so influential, it is important to ascertain whether Cameron's findings are still valid today.

Several other studies round out the early era of shoplifting research. In the early 1960s, Gerald Robin (1963) reported on an analysis of shoplifting apprehension records from three Philadelphia department stores. Another study, by George Won and George Yamamoto (1968), looked at Hawaiian supermarket shoplifting apprehension records for a one-year period. Hilary Bennett (1968) examined data on shoplifters from an industrial community in England. His study is one of the few to look at shoplifters who were referred to the police. Finally, there is the study by J. F. Brady and J. G. Mitchell (1971) of shoplifting apprehensions in a department store in Melbourne, Australia. As is apparent from the international flavor of these studies, shoplifting has been a concern around the world.

LIMITATIONS AND STRENGTHS OF STORE APPREHENSION DATA

Before proceeding, it is important to be aware of the shortcoming of store apprehension data. There are four major limitations. First, security

personnel and sociologists agree that most shoplifters are not apprehended by store personnel. With many stores emphasizing self-service
merchandizing, customers/shoplifters have easy access to most merchandise and few clerks or security personnel are monitoring in-store
behavior. Consequently, only a very small proportion of shoplifters are
apprehended. This has led analysts to conclude that apprehension statistics may tell us more about store security personnel practices and
biases than what the population of shoplifters looks like (e.g., Murphy,
1986). Second, often only limited information is obtained from and about
the shoplifter because store records are collected by store personnel
instead of social scientists. Usually, little more than the sex, age, dollar
value of the item(s), and theft technique is recorded. Information on
factors such as social class, family relationships, prior criminal involvements, and motivations, which are of interest to sociologists, is rarely
obtained systematically. Researchers could alleviate this problem by
working with store security managers to incorporate relevant questions,
and by training security personnel on how to improve their data collection techniques. Third, information obtained from the person apprehended, especially on motives and intentions, is likely to be of
questionable validity due to the subject's immediate and impending legal
predicament. The crisis situation tends to encourage statements that are
often crafted to minimize the consequences the individual faces and are
not dedicated to an accurate sharing of information. A security officer
provided me with an example in which she doubted an apprehended
shoplifter's claim that she had simply "forgotten to pay for the item."
Because the item that the suspect had worn out of the store was a
brassiere, the security officer did not believe the suspect's claim.

Fourth, patterns derived from the records compiled by one store are
not necessarily generalizable to other stores. Each store attracts and
serves particular types of customers, and probably also certain types of
shoplifters (Espinosa, 1989). A hardware store, for example, will attract
more male shoppers/shoplifters, while an upscale boutique will be more
appealing to females. Therefore, it is risky to generalize findings from
one store to all other stores. Being cognizant of this problem, researchers
have tended to concentrate their studies on department stores and supermarkets. They have done this because of the large volume of sales
and shoplifting taking place in these establishments, and also because
a wide cross-section of the population (e.g., social classes and ages)
patronize (buy and steal from) these types of retail establishments. This
strategy is reasonable but it does ignore shoplifting done in the many
small stores and specialty retail establishments. Future research should
explore how shoplifters from these types of retail establishments differ
from those apprehended in large supermarkets and department stores.

On the other hand, store records can provide some accurate types of data about individuals apprehended for shoplifting. Characteristics such as sex and age can be easily recorded by store personnel. Likewise, the dollar value, number and type of item(s) taken, and theft techniques are available and can be accurately recorded. Store records also include very good data on how the store deals with the apprehended shoplifter. Typically, stores will record whether the person is released, if police were called in, and if there was legal action. These statistics are useful starting points for the analysis of shoplifting, shoplifters, and how stores deal with them.

LIMITATIONS AND STRENGTHS OF SELF-REPORT AND INTERVIEW DATA

Given the limitations of store apprehension data, researchers have sought the cooperation of shoplifters. More quantitative researchers have employed self-report questionnaires, and qualitative researchers have relied on interviews. Both of these methods can "fill in" much of the information that is absent from store record studies. The limitations are that the researcher is dependent on the respondent's (1) ability to recall information; and (2) willingness to accurately convey information to the researcher. The recall problem can be alleviated by focusing on recent time periods. The honesty problem can be minimized by guaranteeing the respondent anonymity and by gaining their trust prior to data collection. There are also problems of obtaining good samples of respondents. The early Chicago School sociologists promoted the life history (one delinquent's own story) approach. Other researchers, however, concluded that generating a book per subject was not an economical research strategy. Contemporary researchers (e.g., Katz, 1988; Johnson et al., 1985) typically interview small samples of subjects, which still impose limits on how far their results can be generalized. Self-report researchers obtain even larger samples (e.g., Klemke, 1982a; Cox et al., 1990), but often they are not random samples. Even though there are quite a few interview and self-report studies, they are primarily focused on youth (often in small communities and of students) and/or heroin street addicts. Very few exist on adults (particularly female adults) or on middle-class shoplifters. This is mainly because researchers perceive that these kinds of people will be less eager to participate in this type of research. Several studies verify the difficulty of obtaining adult cooperation (Ray, 1987; Kallis and Vanier, 1985).

These problems need to be kept in mind when analyzing interview and self-report research. Nevertheless, these methods often are the *only* ways that data on many facets of shoplifting can be obtained. Therefore, it is vital that these types of research continue and be improved. This contemporary analysis of shoplifting is very dependent on data generated by researchers utilizing these types of research methods.

In the following sections, various demographic variables will be explored to see how they relate to shoplifting. The early-era shoplifting studies will be examined first. Then, more recent store apprehension studies will be considered; finally, self-report and interview studies will be woven into the analysis. Ideally, a review of the accumulated descriptive research would result in a profile of the kinds of people that are more likely to be shoplifters. Obviously, the more distinctive a profile is, the more value it would have for store security personnel and social scientists seeking to understand this type of behavior. The quest for a descriptive profile of the shoplifter will be initiated by examining how shoplifting is patterned across the life cycle.

AGE AND SHOPLIFTING

Many types of crime and deviance show significant patterns in terms of when they are most likely to occur in the life cycle. Hugh Cline (1980) conducted an extensive analysis of how criminal activity varied throughout the life cycle. For example, he found that youth were more active in property crimes (auto theft, burglary, and larceny), while drunkenness and gambling were offenses committed by middle-aged individuals. Shoplifting activity also appears to change dramatically as individuals age. The early-era store record studies consistently found that young people were more likely to be apprehended for shoplifting than were older people. While Cameron (1964) did not give precise numbers, she did present a population pyramid graph (in five-year age intervals) that portrayed male and female apprehension patterns for Lakeside Co. Visual inspection of this graph revealed dramatic peaks for both males and females in the under–20 age groups. For males, apprehensions were most frequent in the 10–14 age group, followed by a slightly smaller number in the 15–19 age group. The pattern for females was highest in the 15–19 age group. While apprehensions for males dropped off sharply in the over–20 age groups, female apprehensions remained quite high until age 55 and then declined.

The other early-era studies also confirmed that young persons were more likely to be apprehended for shoplifting. Table 3.1 presents summary data from several of these studies. As can be seen, there is a high degree of consensus that individuals under age 20 are most likely to be apprehended for shoplifting. This pattern was particularly strong in the department store studies conducted by Robin (1963) and Brady and Mitchell (1971). It was also evident in Bennett's (1968) analysis of police records (not shown in Table 3.1). Compared to these studies, Won and

Table 3.1
Age of Individuals Apprehended for Shoplifting in Early-Era Studies
(in percentages)

Age	Robin	Brady & Mitchell		Won & Yamamoto
	Supermarkets	Department Stores		Department Stores
		Males	Females	
0-19	62.67	73.4	55.9	32.0
20-29	12.9	7.0	16.8	22.6
30-39	9.1	5.9	10.6	17.5
40-49	5.74	4.0	7.4	14.9
50-59	5.5	6.3	4.1	6.9
60-69	2.9	3.6	6.0	6.1
70+	0.8			
Total Number	1,115	225	369	493

Sources: Derived from Gerald D. Robin (1963), "Patterns of Department Store Shoplifting"
(*Crime and Delinquency* 9(April): 168); George Won and George Yamamoto
(1968), "Social Structure and Deviant Behavior: A Study of Shoplifting" (*Sociology
and Social Research* 53: 47); and J. F. Brady and J. G. Mitchell (1971), "Shoplifting
in Melbourne" (*Australian and New Zealand Journal of Criminology* 4(September):
156).

Yamamoto (1968) found that a smaller percentage of Hawaiian supermarket shoplifters were under age 20 and that more were middle-aged.

Data from recent store apprehension studies are shown in Table 3.2.
The Commercial Services Systems Inc. data (Griffin, 1988) from 391
southern Californian supermarkets is similar to the Hawaiian supermarket study in showing a somewhat older age for those apprehended.
This is not surprising, as supermarkets contain fewer items that are
appealing to children or adolescents. The other data set shown in Table
3.2 was obtained by Klemke. These statistics constitute all the apprehensions made in a multi-state department store chain for the last half
of 1989 and all of 1990. As in the early-era department store studies,
over half of those apprehended for shoplifting were under age 20.
Slightly more young males were apprehended than females. Otherwise,
there are only minor gender differences. After the peak in the 11–15 age

Table 3.2
Age of Individuals Apprehended for Shoplifting in Two Recent Studies
(in percentages)

| Commercial Service Systems: Supermarkets | | Klemke: Multi-state Department Stores | | |
Age		Age	Males	Females
Under 12	3.4	Under 10	7.6	3.8
12-17	12.7	11-15	35.0	29.7
18-29	34.5	16-20	18.8	10.0
		21-30	15.2	20.9
30-39	24.0	31-40	12.5	15.9
40-49	10.0	41-50	6.4	5.0
50-59	6.3	51-60	2.0	2.4
60+	8.8	61+	2.5	3.2
Total Number	9,832		4,807	2,627

Sources: Roger Griffin (1988), *25th Annual Report: Shoplifting in Supermarkets* (Van Nuys, Calif.: Commercial Service Systems, Inc.: 11); and Lloyd W. Klemke, data collected for this book.

group, apprehensions generally decreased throughout the rest of the life cycle.[1]

Finally, Murphy (1986) looked at the age distribution of 75,833 individuals who had been *convicted* of shoplifting in England in 1981. This study discovered that about one-third were under age 20. Most of those convicted were middle-aged shoplifters, and only 14 percent were over age 50. Because these statistics are products of screening by store and legal personnel (constituting data on apprehended shoplifters who are considered to be more serious cases deserving prosecution), they must be viewed with caution.

With the exception of the British data, all these official statistic studies show a clear inverse relationship between age and shoplifting. This pattern was especially strong in department store studies compared to those done in supermarkets. This may mean that youth, in fact, do shoplift more than their adult counterparts. However, it is also plausible that youth get caught more frequently than adults because they are watched more carefully by store personnel, or because they shoplift less proficiently than adults. Self-report data will help resolve this issue.

Unfortunately, only a few self-report studies present extensive data on shoplifting. While very few of these studies sample adults, several do provide good data on shoplifting patterns in the early part of the life cycle. One of these is the research conducted by Klemke (1978a; 1978b; 1982a; 1982b). The study of juvenile shoplifting in several small communities provides the most comprehensive set of self-report data in the shoplifting literature. The analysis of the shoplifting activity, conducted during the short lives of these high school respondents, revealed an interesting pattern. Most of the crime-delinquency literature, relying on *Uniform Crime Reports* statistics, identifies *late* adolescence as the most criminogenic period of the life cycle. The data in Table 3.3, however, indicate that more individuals reported shoplifting when they were *under age 10* and also that the frequency of shoplifting declined as they got older (Klemke, 1978b). These conclusions might be questioned because different time frames are used for the different age periods (e.g., the last period is only about eight months).

Additional data from this study, however, reinforce the original conclusion. For example, younger high school students reported more involvement in recent shoplifting (during the past eight months of the school year) than did the older students: 38.8 percent of the freshmen reported shoplifting during the last school year, compared to 25 percent of the sophomores, 19 percent of the juniors, and 17.7 of the seniors.[2] In addition, 73.8 percent of the 751 high school shoplifters began shoplifting prior to age 10; 22.8 percent began between age 10 and the last school year; and only 3.4 percent began during the last school year. These findings suggest that shoplifting may be done by fewer youth as they move into and through the adolescent years.

While only limited data are available, it is quite likely that even though fewer older adolescents and adults are shoplifting, they are probably taking more expensive items. Therefore, they may constitute a more serious problem to the retail community. This pattern was evident in the apprehension data collected by Klemke from the multi-state department stores. For example, 72 percent of those who were nine year's old when apprehended had taken items valued at less than $10. But only 47 percent of the 15-year-old and 21 percent of the 20-year-old apprehended shoplifters had taken items valued at less than $10.

The only national self-report glimpse of age trends in shoplifting beyond the high school years comes from the major study, *Monitoring the Future* (Osgood et al., 1989). This national survey of high school seniors tracked samples of the original respondents until they reached age 23.

Table 3.3
Frequency of Shoplifting Activity by Age and Sex (in percentages)

	Never	1	2-4	5-10	11+	N*
While under Age 10						
Males	46.5	20.3	18.1	6.8	8.3	(557)
Females	57.3	24.3	13.4	2.6	2.4	(557)
Between Age 10 and the Beginning of This School Year						
Males	54.9	15.9	13.5	5.3	10.4	(561)
Females	70.4	7.4	10.0	5.3	6.9	(582)
Since School Began This School Year *(Almost Nine Months)*						
Males	72.7	11.6	7.4	3.0	5.3	(569)
Females	80.3	8.6	6.0	1.6	3.6	(580)

*The total number of responses varies slightly because of non-response to certain questions.
Source: Lloyd W. Klemke (1978), "Reassessment of the Adolescent Crime Wave Model" (*California Sociologist* 1(2): 184).

One of the self-report offenses inquired about was shoplifting activity. This study provides the best national data on the scope of shoplifting activity. It is limited only in that (1) an interesting segment of the population, high school dropouts, are excluded; (2) it covers only a small segment of the life cycle; and (3) it does not pursue any sophisticated analysis that targets shoplifting behavior. Table 3.4 presents the data on the respondents' shoplifting activity for the last year. To obtain a count of the number of shoplifting offenses, respondents were asked to check one of the following response categories: "not at all," "once," "twice," "three or four times," or "five or more times." An individual's shoplifting was counted according to the number checked. Individuals checking "five or more," however, were given a score of five even though they may have actually shoplifted a much larger number of times. This procedure obviously undercounts the number of offenses, but it was utilized

Table 3.4
Self-Reported Illegal Behavior by Age and Sex

		Number of Offenses Reported per 1,000						
Sex	Offense	17	18	AGE 19	20	21	22	23
Males								
	Shoplifting	831	613	465	385	370	188	245
	Aggression Sum	993	765	451	497	233	389	173
	Property Sum	3,420	2,818	1,874	1,901	1,501	1,206	945
Females								
	Shoplifting	536	388	319	207	161	215	137
	Aggression Sum	368	281	261	145	142	101	124
	Property Sum	1,553	1,117	1,037	744	615	677	452

		Percentage Reporting One or More Offenses						
Males								
	Shoplifting	39.0	28.8	22.8	16.4	19.4	10.4	11.5
	Any Aggressive Offense	34.9	28.0	21.8	20.6	13.8	17.0	8.7
	Any Property Offense	68.5	59.6	47.8	46.4	42.1	31.0	27.7
Females								
	Shoplifting	26.6	18.2	15.4	12.7	8.0	11.8	7.0
	Any Aggressive Offense	19.5	15.0	14.6	9.3	8.5	5.4	9.3
	Any Property Offense	45.0	34.7	29.3	28.3	18.9	22.7	16.8

Source: Adapted from Table 1 and Table 2 in Wayne D. Osgood et al. (1984) "Time Trends and Age Trends in Arrests and Self-Reported Illegal Behavior" (*Criminology* 27(3): 397, 398).

by the researchers to avoid distorting the total figures by a few very active offenders. Analysis of this table reveals that shoplifting declined (both in the number of offenses and also in that fewer individuals reported recent shoplifting) as the respondents matured from age 17 to the ripe old age of 23. The decline occurred for both males and females. Table 3.4 also shows data for summary indexes of the respondents' aggressive offenses and property offenses. Both of these clusters of crimes show a decrease in frequency as age increased, mirroring the trend just identified for shoplifting activity.

Additional confirmation of this pattern, for the ages covered in the *Monitoring the Future* study, comes from data I obtained from a university bookstore. During a five-year period (1984–1989), 607 individuals were apprehended for shoplifting. It is not surprising that 78.4 percent of those apprehended were students. While age and year in school are not perfectly correlated, typically upper-class students are older than those beginning college. A clear pattern emerged indicating that more freshmen were apprehended than upper-class students. Specifically, the percentages of apprehended students, by their year in school, were as follows: 38.3 percent freshmen, 19.9 percent sophomores, 18 percent juniors, 11.6 percent seniors, and 12.2 percent graduate students. Only freshmen were over-represented, compared to their proportion of the student body of the school.

Finally, a large self-report study (Tittle, 1980) of adults in three states (New Jersey, Iowa, and Oregon) provides some interesting data. While it did not target shoplifting behavior per se, it did include questions on general theft behavior during the last five years. Specifically, the respondents were asked if they had taken something worth $5, and another question asked about the theft of something worth about $50. Self-reported theft behavior (done within the past five years) was found to decline dramatically as age increased. For example, $5 thefts were reported by 46 percent of those age 15–24, by 23 percent of those age 25–44, by 10 percent of those age 45–65, and by only 2 percent of those over age 65 (Tittle, 1980: 90). This declining pattern was also evident for $50 thefts and seven other types of criminal and deviant behavior. These statistics lend credence to Michael Gottfredson and Travis Hirschi's (1990) controversial "invariance thesis," which holds that crime declines with age everywhere and at all times.

Turning to the last phase of the life cycle, there has been a popular notion that a great deal of shoplifting is done by the elderly (Grosswirth, 1981; Feinberg, 1984a). This perception appears to be unwarranted when one examines store apprehension statistics. Looking at the early-era studies (see Table 3.1) and more recent apprehension studies (see Table 3.2), it is clear that individuals over age 60 are less likely to be apprehended than almost any other age group. The only self-report study to explore the involvement of theft behavior for an elderly age group is Tittle's (1980). As just reported, only 2 percent of those over age 65 reported $5 thefts during the last five years. Several studies devoted to the elderly shoplifter have reported increases in the number of arrests among elderly citizens (Feinberg, 1984b: Fyfe, 1984; Curran, 1984; Moak et al., 1988). This increase is partly due to the fact that more people are living longer. Fyfe (1984), however, feels that much of the increase is an artifact of the trend that merchants are more willing to apprehend the elderly shoplifter today than they were 20 years ago. Even though more elderly people are being arrested today, they are still much less likely to be arrested than other age groups (Curran, 1984; Wilbanks, 1984). Murphy (1986) also noted that only 5.9 percent of 72,956 found guilty of shoplifting in England were in the over-60 age group. Thus, all of the store apprehension studies as well as self-report, arrest, and conviction statistics confirm that shoplifting is not a major problem in the later phases of the life cycle.

In summary, there is a great deal of consensus that shoplifting is most frequent in the early part of the life cycle and that it declines as individuals move through the life cycle. Confirmation of this pattern by self-report studies suggests that the high percentage of youth in store apprehension studies is not simply a product of store biases or practices. What happens to shoplifting activity in the middle phases of the life cycle is a bit more problematic. Some of the store apprehension studies suggest, particularly for females, that there may be relatively high levels of shoplifting during the middle-aged segment of the life cycle. Historically, as was mentioned in Chapter 2, this pattern was analyzed by Abelson (1989b) and O'Brien (1983). More recently, Cameron found large numbers of female apprehensions in the 35–55 age group. Likewise, the supermarket studies showed shoplifting apprehensions to be fairly high in the 20–40 age group (Won and Yamamoto, 1968; Griffin, 1988), and this was also evident in Klemke's multi-state department store statistics. On the other hand, the limited adult self-report data on shoplifting and general theft behavior show consistent declines as age increases. Because of the potential biases in store apprehension data, I am inclined to put more weight on the limited self-report data. Finally, all the data suggest that shoplifting is at a low level during the last phase of the life cycle. Therefore, it appears that shoplifting is inversely related to age and exemplifies Gottfredson and Hirschi's invariance thesis.

GENDER AND SHOPLIFTING

Perhaps no other demographic variable has produced as much misplaced confidence and misleading information about shoplifting patterns as gender. The popular stereotype is that females are more frequently involved in shoplifting than are males. Prostitution and shoplifting have been considered to be the crimes of choice of females. This view has a long history, as the research by Abelson (1989b) and O'Brien (1983) testifies. Lombroso, writing in the late 1800s, articulated a similar position when he described some shoplifters as "occasional criminals" and others as "born criminals" (see Booster Box 1).

BOOSTER BOX 1
LOMBROSO'S TYPES OF SHOPLIFTERS

Occasional Shoplifters

Shoplifting, which has become so common since the era of huge establishments, is a specially feminine offence—temptation being furnished by the immense number of articles exhibited, and which excite the desires of women who can only afford to buy a few. We saw that fine things are not articles of luxury for women, but articles of necessity, since they equip them for conquest; and therefore the huge shop, with its manifold and various seductions, betrays them into crime. . . . Ladies who cannot spend, or do not need to do so, go all the same to the great sales, as an engineer will go to an exhibition of machines, just out of interested curiosity. Little by little a fever possesses them, and they either buy beyond their means or accomplish a dexterous theft.

Louise C., An Example of Lombroso's *Born Criminal* Type

Louise C. (Magnum writes of her), aged nine, was the daughter of a mad father, always in a condition of sexual excitement. She was of weak intelligence; her instincts had always been bad, her conduct turbulent, and her mind incapable of concentration.

At age three she was a thief, and laid hands on her mother's money, articles in shops, on everything, in short that came her way. At five she was arrested and conveyed to the police-office, after a determined resistance. Her habits were vagabond and unruly. She shrieked, tore off her stockings, threw her dolls into the gutter, lifted up her skirts in the street.

Magnum asserts that she has no morbid peculiarity of face; but on looking at her photograph, one perceives that, although only nine years old, she offers the exact type of the born criminal. Her physiognomy is Mongolian, her jaws and cheek-bones are immense; the frontal sinuses strong, the nose flat, with a prognathous under-jaw, asymmetry of face, and above all, precocity and virility of expression. She looks like a grown woman—nay, a man.

Source: Ceasar Lombroso and William Ferrero, 1898. *The Female Offender.*
New York: D. Appleton: 206–7; 99.

More recently, Freda Adler (1975) analyzed the sources of female crime
and how they have been changing. She noted that the traditional woman
homemaker often faced limited financial resources and career options.
Females were frequently tied to the home except for routine shopping
trips to acquire the family's staples and extras. These conditions made
it an easy transition from woman as the shopper to woman as the shoplifter. Adler highlights a typical financial dilemma experienced by females in the case of Marge, who was left to support her two children
after her husband deserted the family. Having no vocational training,
she became a barmaid in a restaurant-lounge and considered resorting
to prostitution like a co-worker was doing. Feeling uncomfortable with
this option because of her religious upbringing, and not possessing a
very desirable figure, she resorted to other ways of alleviating her financial plight. Her transformation into a shoplifter and then a bank
robber is described by Adler in Booster Box 2.

BOOSTER BOX 2
MARGE THE BOOSTER

In place of prostitution, Marge found a more acceptable degree
of reprehensibility in shoplifting. "Boosting" from department
stores became a regular habit with her. At first she began by
putting small items, like watches, into her pocket. Later she
progressed to more sophisticated methods. She wore large baggy
coats which could conceal things like toasters and radios, then
began to sew large bag-like pockets inside the coats to facilitate
even larger load handling. She shoplifted for years, and was only
caught once. On that occasion she was allowed to go free on
her own recognizance and, although threatened with further
prosecution, never heard of the incident again.

Five years ago Marge robbed her first bank. The planning took
her some months. "It was something that came to me all of a
sudden. I had a couple of big debts and was getting tired of
working like I was. I wanted a bit of easy time. I mean, the kids
were getting older and I was still working and after all those
years, I needed a break."

Source: Freda Adler. 1975. *Sisters in Crime: The Rise of the New Female Criminal.* New York: McGraw-Hill: 6–7.

Articles in popular magazines, aimed at a female audience, regularly foster the viewpoint that shoplifting is a female offense.[3] Likewise, social scientists often claim that females are more active shoplifters than males. Cameron's data are usually cited as evidence of this pattern. She found that 60 percent of those apprehended in the Lakeside Co. department store were females and a dramatic 83 percent of the apprehended adults were females.

Other early-era studies also confirmed that a higher percentage of females were apprehended for shoplifting. Robin's data from three department stores showed that 60.7 percent of those apprehended were females (53.4% in store A, 73.9% in store B, and 41.5% in store C). Both Won and Yamamoto's research of Hawaiian supermarkets and Brady and Mitchell's study of a Melbourne department store found that 60 percent of the apprehended shoplifters were females. Finally, Bennett's (1968) analysis of shoplifters reported to the police in Midtown, England, also found that 56.6 percent were females. One bias that may be operating in many of these studies comes from the possibility that the gender of the person doing the apprehending may influence the likelihood of being apprehended. As many store sales and security personnel are female, they may feel more comfortable observing and following, and less threatened when confronting, individuals of the same gender. Even with this caveat, the high level of consensus in historical works and the early-era studies seems to establish that females are more active shoplifters than males.

However, questions arise when more recent studies and particularly when self-report data are examined. A major source of data for supermarkets, collected by Commercial Services Systems Inc. (Griffin, 1988). revealed that 44.2 percent of 9,832 shoplifters apprehended in 1987 were females. The percentages for adults and juveniles were very similar. For each year between 1976 and 1987, the data showed that from 41.6 percent to 50.9 percent of those apprehended were females. In only one of these years, 1980, were more females (50.9%) apprehended than males. The multi-state department store data (see Table 3.2) show that 64 percent of those apprehended were males. Data on this issue, from the university bookstore mentioned earlier, are presented in Table 3.5. Because this is a more specialized store catering to a university population, it offers an interesting point of comparison. For each of the five years covered in the study, males were clearly more likely to be apprehended. Overall, 70.5 percent of the apprehended shoplifters were male and 29.5 percent were females, even though males constitute slightly less than 60 percent of the student body.

Unfortunately, the FBI's *Uniform Crime Reports* do not present gender statistics for shoplifting. Various researchers have analyzed samples of shoplifters that have been referred to the police. These studies provide

Table 3.5
Apprehensions for Shoplifting in a University Bookstore by Sex (in percentages)

School Year	Males	Females	Number
1984-85	78	22	(22)
1985-86	69	31	(145)
1986-87	74	26	(180)
1987-88	54	46	(79)
1988-89	72	28	(112)
TOTALS	71	29	(607)

Source: Lloyd W. Klemke, data collected for this book.

another point of comparison for gender patterns. Moore (1984), for example, studied 300 shoplifters being prosecuted for shoplifting in a municipal court of a medium-sized American city. He found that 56 percent of these individuals were males.

Several crosscultural studies of police statistics report gender patterns for shoplifting. Most interesting is a study of crime in the Netherlands (Bruinsma et al., 1984). Researchers found that the number of female shoplifters reported to the police increased from 1,960 in 1962 to 5,894 in 1976 (3 times as many) but the male numbers rose from 700 in 1962 to 5,121 in 1976 (7.3 times as many). They link the larger increase in male shoplifting to the increased involvement in shopping by males. Across the English Channel, D. P. Walsh (1978) found that males were slightly more likely to be found among those reported to the police for shoplifting in Exeter, England. Daniel Murphy looked at all of the British court proceedings for shoplifting in 1981. This revealed that 58.5 percent of the 83,202 shoplifting cases taken to court were males (Murphy, 1986: 206).

Finally, self-report studies bearing on gender differences supply further evidence on this issue. The first self-report study coincides with the time frame covered by the early-era studies. This is Martin Gold's (1970) study of 13- to 15-year-old youth in Flint, Michigan. The youth were interviewed in the early 1960s. In contrast to the early-era apprehension studies, Gold found that males committed about 75 percent of the reported acts of shoplifting. More recently,

Table 3.6
Percentage Responding Yes to "Have You Ever" Questions

	White Males	Black Males	White Females	Black Females
Taken little things (worth less than $2) from a store	62.8	52.4	55.8	37.2
Taken things worth between $10 and $50 from a store	13.5	14.2	14.2	15.2
Taken things of large value (worth more than $50) from a store	5.2	5.6	1.4	3.7
Been caught shoplifting by the clerk or owner of a store	32.8	29.3	23.8	23.8

Source: Adapted from Appendix B in Michael J. Hindelang et al. (1981), *Measuring Delinquency* (Beverly Hills, Calif.: Sage Publications: 223–24).

Lloyd Klemke's (1982a) data from high school students in small communities revealed that 70 percent of the males had shoplifted compared to 57.1 percent of the females. Klemke's data in Table 3.3 indicate that males also reported doing more shoplifting during all three age periods (in high school).

A complementary look at shoplifting by youth in a large metropolitan area is provided by Michael Hindelang et al. (1981). They conducted a major self-report study of a representative sample of youth in Seattle. Table 3.6 presents the percentages of youth who admitted committing various dollar values of shoplifting activity, by sex and race. Males reported more shoplifting of items under $2 in value and items over $50, but similar levels of involvement to females in taking items worth $10 to $50. These patterns were evident for both white and black respondents.

The *Monitoring the Future* national data (see Table 3.4) also show that more males reported shoplifting and committed a greater number of shoplifting acts during the last year. Additional data from this large longitudinal study show that the pattern has been repeated in each sample of high school seniors that have been surveyed between 1977 and 1989 (Flanagan and Maguire, 1990). Two self-report studies of large samples of students in Georgia found that juvenile males sho-plifted more than juvenile females (Moschis, 1987; Cox et al., 1990).

Ray (1987) conducted a study of shoppers at various shopping centers in Spokane, Washington. An extensive questionnaire and a stamped return envelope were passed out to randomly selected shoppers who said they would cooperate with the study. Unfortunately, only 38.2 percent returned a completed questionnaire. This makes it difficult to have much confidence in the sample. The researcher also does not give the statistics but only states that males and females reported similar rates of shoplifting. In addition, several self-report studies of college students detected more shoplifting by males than by females (Kraut, 1976; El Dirghami, 1974). The only other self-report evidence on adults is Charles Tittle's (1980) study. As mentioned earlier, general theft questions were utilized rather than specific shoplifting items. Tittle found that 30 percent of the males but only 14 percent of the females reported committing a $5 theft in the past five years. Similarly, 10 percent of the males but only 4 percent of the females reported committing a $50 theft. These gender differences persisted even when Tittle controlled for age, socioeconomic status, and race.

In summary, the historical sources and the early-era store apprehen-sion studies showed that females were more likely to be shoplifters than males. On the other hand, almost all the post–1970 studies of official data and all the self-report data show that males were equally or more active in shoplifting. Therefore, the evidence appears to overwhelmingly support the conclusion that males are typically more active in shoplifting than females. Because females continue to be very involved in con-sumption responsibilities, they will continue to be very evident in shop-lifting statistics. For certain types of stores and places they may even have higher rates than males. Likewise, shoplifting will continue to be one of the more popular types of crime (more so than burglary or rob-bery) for females.

RACE, ETHNICITY, AND FOREIGNER STATUS AND SHOPLIFTING

Sociologists have often noted that individuals who are racially or cul-turally distinct (i.e., ethnic minorities or foreigners) may be more prone to exhibit deviant behavior because of different life-styles or because of prejudice and discrimination. A search of the shoplifting literature un-covered very little research on these variables. This can be attributed, in part, to the belief of store officials that these are sensitive topics. Therefore, stores may not collect this data; if they do, they may be reluctant to release it for public information. Nevertheless, there are several suggestive studies on these variables.

Cameron (1964) explored racial patterns, but it should be noted that her data were obtained prior to the civil rights era and are probably out of date on this particular issue. She found that blacks were under-represented in store apprehension statistics (only 10.2%) when compared to their proportion of the Chicago population (15%). It is interesting that while 58 percent of the blacks apprehended for shoplifting were formally charged, only 10.9 percent of the whites were so charged (Cameron, 1964). This pattern, plus the fact that blacks were apprehended for stealing less expensive items, led her to conclude that a significant racial bias was operating. Robin's research (1963) on department store apprehensions in Philadelphia, conducted in the same era as Cameron's study, noted that 48.2 percent of the apprehended shoplifters were black. Furthermore, he also found that black shoplifters were more likely to be prosecuted (79.2%) than were white shoplifters (62.1%).

The only early-era study to look at ethnic distinctions was Won and Yamamoto's research on Hawaiian supermarket apprehension data. The most significant pattern detected was a higher rate of shoplifting apprehensions for Hawaiians (25.9%) compared to their proportion of the population (15.1%) (Won and Yamamoto, 1968: 52). The authors point to the possible importance of the lower economic status of this minority group. It is surprising that they do not suggest that discrimination might be affecting the statistics.

Recent store apprehension studies are also reluctant to raise racial or ethnic issues. Even the otherwise good data on supermarket shoplifters provided by Commercial Services System Inc. (Griffin, 1988) does not present any statistics on race or ethnicity. While quantitative studies are scarce, there is a useful ethnographic study of British store detectives by Murphy. His interviews and field observations revealed that store detectives made many statements that blacks, Asians, Middle Easterners, and generally all foreign tourists were more likely to be viewed with suspicion (Murphy, 1986).[4] He did not produce specific or systematic evidence that these attitudes resulted in discriminatory practices. But he did indicate that there is great potential for self-fulfilling prophecies to occur, as these beliefs influence the perceptions and actions of store detectives. The difficulty of separating the impact of biased perceptions from objective assessments of behavior is poignantly evident in a journalist's account of a personal experience. Because of the complexity of the situation, all of his lengthy description is presented in Booster Box 3.

Booster Box 3
"A FACE-OFF WITH RACISM: IN A MANHATTAN TRAIN
STATION, GRAPPLING WITH THE TRICKY QUESTIONS OF
PREJUDICE AND RACE RELATIONS"

The glassed-in booth is located at a busy corner of the esplanade
in Pennsylvania Station, where I am rushing to catch a train from
Manhattan back home to Long Island. It is the afternoon of my
son's birthday, and I still don't have a suitable gift, and now the
store, with its Spartan neon sign, "T-Shirts," catches my eye. In
the stifling heat of a summer afternoon, the shop is suddenly
transformed from cramped dinginess into an oasis of light and
relief. I enter.

Inside, I note that the proprietors, two Asian women and an
elderly Asian man, are watching me. Very closely. I pull some
shirts from the shelves, inspecting fabric and stitching, when one
of the women gets up and walks over. Standing watch with arms
folded on her chest, she asks, "What do you want?" Is she talking
to me? She has an edge in her voice that could cut steel. "Do
you have money?" I am dressed in a business suit. My shoes are
from Brooks Brothers. No matter. I have brown skin, and this
seems to invite her suspicions. I shift into my Prejudice Response
Mode, hoping I do not betray the fact that, despite the frequency
of my encounters with prejudice like this, I am always a little bit
shocked and hurt. I feel, despite myself, like the thief she may
take me to be. I ask the price of the T-shirt. "That shirt costs
$13," she says. Next move, I look at one shirt I like. The fabric
feels soft to the touch. Once again, I have offended the saleswoman, who jars me again by rubbing the shirt as though I have
dirtied it. Refolding the shirt, my saleslady curtly wheels around
and takes her place behind the counter. I've been through these
absurdities before. So often, in fact, that it fails to surprise now.
I remind myself of Ambrose Bierce's definition of patience: A
minor form of despair disguised as virtue.

After completing the transaction—in cash, of course, and with
the proprietress smiling for the first time—four black teenagers jos-
tle each other through the door. The smile vanishes from my saleslady's face, and she freezes. "What do you want!" she barks. But
now there is another kind of edge in her voice. Her jaw muscles
work so hard they look like they could chew pig iron and spit out
cannonballs. "If you come here to steal, leave right now! Come

on! Get going!'' For emphasis, she grabs a long broomstick from behind the door and waves it at the kids. This is enough. For her to leap to this conclusion, that the four were thieves, seems so gross I feel compelled to speak up. But then the tallest of the crew makes strides for the door. The Asian saleswoman locks it. "You don't have any right to keep me here," he says. "I'm not no criminal. I'm not doing nothing." The saleswoman: "None of you goes until you all go." One of the kids: "We're not doing nothing. You think all black people is thieves. That's just racist." I am about to leap to their defense when the saleswoman next to me grabs the jacket of one of the young men. It opens to reveal one of the T-shirts from the rack. "Look, man," says the kid caught in the act. "See what you did? Playing that trick on me." The kids laugh. Only the old man doesn't think it's so funny, and he responds by grabbing the kids and shoving them outside.

It seems that, on many levels, a contest has been playing itself out, a clash of contending stereotypes, all working themselves out in a stifling atmosphere of bitterness, racial division, fear and rage. Outside the store, the four kids shower the merchants with racial epithets and spit at them: "Dirty Jap," one shouts; another sends gobs of spittle flying toward the shopkeepers. The old man is caught in the face. "Call the cops," says my saleswoman. "Call the cops."

Outside the store, I tell the kids that what they did was stupid and dangerous. "They're just racists," says one kid. I ask: "But what the hell were you doing with the shirt stuffed inside your jacket?" "Oh, man, we was just playing with'em. Just playing." Some joke. I had been ready to defend him, but now I wonder what I would have been defending. In the next moment, the kids are gone.

Back inside the store on the next day, the same saleswoman who had taken out the stick recognizes me. "Oh, hello," she says, almost friendly. When I ask about the incident, she says, "You have no idea about this place. The kids come in here, a whole group of them, and while you watch one, the other grabs a shirt or a sweater or a whole bunch of shirts and sweaters, and runs out the door, whoosh!" I tell her I sympathize with the pressure she must feel, being in a shop like this 10, 12 hours each day, but that's hardly an excuse for prejudice. "Black people come and try to steal," she says. But do whites come in to steal, too? Yes, she says, but it is the blacks whom you have to watch. "You have to be careful with them." So much for reason. In such an atmosphere, is it reasonable to hope we can achieve racial harmony?

Source: Scott Minerbrook. 1988. "A Face-Off with Racism: In a Manhattan Train
Station, Grappling with the Tricky Questions of Prejudice and Race Relations."
U.S. News & World Report 105(August 22): 57.

Several studies have attempted to assess racial bias after a shoplifting
suspect has been apprehended (Cameron, 1964; Cohen and Stark, 1974;
Hindelang, 1974; Lundman, 1978). These studies are primarily focused
on analyzing factors that influence the decision to call the police and
arrest the apprehended shoplifter. They will be analyzed more extensively in Chapter 6, and therefore are only briefly summarized here.
Cameron did find a very significant racial bias against blacks in her early
study. As mentioned earlier, she specifically found that a much larger
proportion of apprehended black shoplifters were referred to the police.
Studies by Lawrence Cohen and Rodney Stark and by Michael Hindelang, on the other hand, concluded that once the dollar value of the
stolen item was taken into account, the decision to arrest was not racially
biased. Thus, the higher black arrest rate was due to blacks stealing
more expensive items. Richard Lundman's research, however, found
that race still played an important role in the decision to refer an apprehended shoplifter to the police.

Finally, self-report studies will be reviewed for what they can tell us
about racial patterns of shoplifting (there are no self-report studies on
ethnicity or foreigner status). Self-report studies have often been done
in communities with small minority populations, thereby limiting their
value on this issue. Nevertheless, there are several studies that explore
the role of racial factors. Gold's study of 13- to 16-year-old youth in Flint,
Michigan, revealed that lower status whites and lower status blacks had
very similar patterns of shoplifting activity. Approximately 60 percent
of both black and white lower status boys reported shoplifting, and
approximately 30 percent of both black and white lower status girls
admitted shoplifting (Gold, 1970).

This finding, that there were no significant racial differences in shoplifting activity, was confirmed in several self-report studies. The national
sample of high school seniors in the *Monitoring the Future* study indicated
almost identical patterns of shoplifting during the 12 years this data has
been collected (Flanagan and Maguire, 1990: 294–95). The Hindelang et
al. self-report study of Seattle youth (see Table 3.6) found only minor
differences between black and white shoplifting patterns. The researchers did qualify their overall conclusions on race-crime patterns because
black official delinquents were more likely to under-report the offenses
that were on their police record (Hindelang et al., 1981). This potential
distortion, however, should not have much impact on the data presented
in Table 3.6. Finally, Tittle's (1980) self-report study on adults in three
states did find that non-whites had higher levels of general theft be-

havior. For example, 29 percent of the non-white respondents reported $5 thefts compared to 20 percent of the whites, and 15 percent of the non-whites reported $50 thefts compared to 6 percent of the whites. Additional data with a racial component can be found in ethnographic and self-report studies of street heroin addicts. These will be reviewed in a following section. Needless to say, more data will be necessary to clarify racial and ethnic patterns of shoplifting. For now, it seems appropriate to conclude that racial and ethnic patterns of who shoplifts, and of how apprehended shoplifters are prosecuted, vary dramatically in different places and times.

SOCIAL CLASS AND SHOPLIFTING

Sociologists have frequently relied on socioeconomic factors as an important variable in their studies of deviant and conforming behavior. In order to establish the utility of this variable it is necessary to show that particular patterns of behavior, such as shoplifting, are more prevalent in certain segments of the social class hierarchy. Unfortunately, the social class data in many shoplifting studies are of questionable quality. There are two main reasons for this. First, store personnel may not collect occupational or income information from apprehended shoplifters. This is particularly true when the suspect is a juvenile. Even when this information is collected, its accuracy is rarely verified. Second, it is very possible that store personnel have social class stereotypes of who should be watched and apprehended (May, 1978: 150). Thus, various types of class biases may influence their behavior and, ultimately, the accuracy of apprehension data. Keeping these problems in mind, let us review the studies that attempt to assess the relationship between social class and shoplifting.

Cameron (1964), for example, utilized a variety of tactics to assess the social class patterns for her Lakeside Co. shoplifters. She obtained information on the occupation of the apprehended shoplifter, or of the husband for the unemployed women shoplifters, from the store records. She was aware that this information was not very precise. In particular, she questioned the validity of the statistic that 41 percent of the apprehended males reported being unemployed. She speculated that males would be reluctant to reveal details about their employment to store security personnel out of fear of jeopardizing their jobs. At any rate, her analysis of the data showed several patterns: (1) Fewer high status persons were apprehended for shoplifting than would be expected (when compared with Chicago census data); and (2) Apprehended shoplifters lived in slightly lower socioeconomic neighborhoods than the typical Lakeside Co. shopper (Cameron, 1964). This conclusion of a slight inverse relationship between social class and shoplifting would be modified to a *strong* inverse relationship for *males*, *if* the data on unemployment were deemed to be accurate.

The other early-era study to concentrate on the social class issue was the study of Hawaiian supermarkets by Won and Yamamoto (1968). Because almost half of those apprehended were students or housewives, the researchers did not feel it was appropriate to look at the income level of the offender. Instead, they relied on various socioeconomic indicators of the offender's neighborhood. Analysis of this type of data makes their conclusions vulnerable to the ecological fallacy, as the offender's social class might be very different from their neighborhood's social class. Nevertheless, they looked at average household income and educational level for the neighborhoods. This revealed that shoplifters were more likely to come from neighborhoods with middle incomes and average levels of education. They also compared the occupation for the head of the household of the shoplifter with the occupational distribution for the population of Honolulu. This analysis revealed that shoplifters were more likely to come from manual labor or working class families.

Because social class data from store apprehension studies are fraught with problems and most do not even present social class data, self-report research would be extremely helpful. Regrettably, there is not a very large pool of studies. Several of the studies that are available, however, do provide some insight into this issue. One of these is Gold's research on 13- to 16-year-old youth in Flint, Michigan. He based his analysis of social class on the father's occupation. His data showed that lower-class white boys and girls reported 10 percent to 20 percent more shoplifting than upper-class whites (Gold, 1970: 77–78).

Klemke's (1982a) study of high school youth used self-report data (of parent's occupations and education levels) to analyze relationships between social class and shoplifting. Table 3.7 shows a slight to moderate inverse relationship between social class and recent shoplifting activity. This relationship became much stronger for females and weaker for males when sex was controlled. Kevin Bales (1982) also found a similar moderate inverse relationship for his high school sample. The finding that lower-class teenagers report somewhat more shoplifting than affluent youth is consistent with Gold's study and most other self-report delinquency research as summarized by Hindelang et al. (1981). Finally, Ray's (1987) research found that three times as many adult shoplifters had low incomes (under $5,000) compared to the non-shoplifters in her random sample of shoppers frequenting Spokane shopping centers. Considering all this evidence, it seems reasonable to tentatively conclude that shoplifting is slightly to moderately more frequent in the lower-class segments of the society. As will be discussed in the next section, shoplifting is much more frequent in certain segments of the "under-

Table 3.7
Frequency of Shoplifting Activity in the Last School Year by Social Class and Sex (in percentages)

Social Class	Never	Low Frequency	Some or Many	Number	Shoplifted Some or Many Times	
					Males	Females
Upper White-Collar	83.4	8.8	7.8	(308)	13.6	2.5
Lower White-Collar	83.5	10.7	5.8	(242)	7.5	3.5
Upper Blue-Collar	72.4	17.9	9.8	(241)	11.0	7.7
Lower Blue-Collar	65.9	17.0	17.0	(227)	16.9	17.7
Unemployed, Retired, and Unclassifiable	67.5	14.6	17.6	(151)	17.5	12.9

Source: Adapted from Table 2 in Lloyd W. Klemke (1982), "Exploring Juvenile Shoplifting" (*Sociology and Social Research* 67 (October): 64).

class." Future researchers will be obligated to confirm the existence of these relationships.

SUBCULTURES AND SHOPLIFTING

Researchers have examined specific subcultures that are thought to be very active in shoplifting. These subcultural studies often concentrate on individuals located in the "underclass," and especially those involved in the street level drug scene. Because of the high level of public concern about how drugs and crime are connected, a great deal of research has been devoted to this topic. Shoplifting has been found to be one of the more frequently committed types of crime within this social world. Recall the accounts of shoplifting by Manny the drug addict, presented in Chapter 2, as a classic example of the intertwining of a drug habit and shoplifting.

Fortunately, there are excellent ethnographic and quantitative self-report studies that provide dramatic documentation of this phenomenon. Alan Sutter's (1969) field study of young addicts in a low-income neighborhood of San Francisco uncovered numerous examples of shoplifting as one of their main types of hustling. Booster Box 4 presents an account from one of his "easy player" respondents (one who specializes in low-risk offenses like selling phony jewelry, pimping, shoplifting, dealing drugs, etc., and uses mainly marijuana and amphetamines).

BOOSTER BOX 4
AN EASY PLAYER

Let me tell you, man, life ain't nothing without weed. When I'm high on weed and I'm looking at my clothes, and I got on $65 shoes and $3 silk socks, and $5 silk shorts, and I go on this bad shark skin slack suit, great big old diamond ring, this omega watch, and I'm loaded off this weed, I'm more aware of how good I really am. I think, "Look how I got this," you know, "I got it hustling," and my mind gets sharp.

Like when I first started, I smoked dope to be happy, yeah, have fun and all. Then I began seeing that weed can do more, you know. Then you see yourself and the way the world really is and the way people be really fronting. That weed makes me aware so I can game. Cause if you're loaded, it seems like you do a lot of things other people can't do. They staggering around from that wine and you feel gooder than they feel and still you can hold your own. I think that they should rename marijuana "future," cause if I get loaded at one o'clock I'm thinking about how I'm going downtown and boost at three o'clock and about them three holes [girls] I got out here. I'm not thinking about the past when I made that hundred dollars yesterday. I may sit down and think: "When I get thirty, I'll own three restaurants, five apartment buildings and three cafes, and I'll have a gang of holes out there." I'm twenty now and I got a long way to go, man. Weed is part of my progress.

Source: Alan G. Sutter. 1969. "Worlds of Drug Use on the Street Scene." In Donald R. Cressey and David A. Ward, eds. *Delinquency, Crime, and Social Process*. New York: Harper & Row: 813.

Other ethnographic and interview studies, such as those conducted by Irving Spergle (1964), Bettylou Valentine (1978), Charles Faupel and Carl

Klockars (1987), and Barbara Lex (1990), refer to shoplifting as one of the "hustles" that is found in lower-class and often racial-ethnic minority communities.

Three of the most significant quantitative self-report projects devoted to this topic have been conducted by James Inciardi (1980), Bruce Johnson et al. (1985), and Gregory Kowalski and Charles Faupel (1990). These research efforts obtained detailed information about the daily lives of street addicts. Inciardi (1980), for example, conducted interviews with 149 female heroin addicts in Miami, Florida (51% white, 34% black, and 15% Hispanic). They revealed extensive involvement in the street culture of drugs-prostitution-shoplifting and other types of crime. When asked to self-report their criminal activity for the last year, the 149 respondents admitted to involvement in a total of 58,708 offenses. The three most frequently committed offenses were prostitution (19,246), drug sales (15,990), and shoplifting (8,713). Two-thirds of the respondents reported being involved in shoplifting. Inciardi also concluded that there was more evidence that criminal activity preceded involvement in drugs than that drugs preceded crime. More recently, Eleanor Miller (1986) studied a similar sample of "street women" in Milwaukee, Wisconsin. Her fascinating ethnographic study also found shoplifting to be part of the hustling repertoires of these economically marginal and predominantly minority females.[5] Clearly, shoplifting has been an important means of enhancing the economic situation of many females who are involved with deviant street networks.

The importance of shoplifting in the street heroin drug subculture was also verified in the field study, *Taking Care of Business* (Johnson et al., 1985). Investigators repeatedly interviewed 201 heroin abusers (many were polydrug users) residing in Harlem. The sample was made up of 55 percent black, 44 percent Hispanic, and 1 percent white residents. Unlike the Inciardi study, Johnson's researchers included both males (75%) and females (25%). The annual income for the respondents averaged about $1,000 from the legitimate economic system. How could they survive and still expend approximately $10,726 a year for various drugs? It is not surprising that the respondents reported an average of about $12,000 in illicit income to help balance their budgets. This resulted in an average total income of $13,000 that was very similar to the income earned by other neighborhood residents working in the licit economic system.

A great deal of specific information was obtained about the criminal involvements of the 201 (150 male and 51 female) heroin users. They were sorted into three categories of heroin usage patterns: 61 were irregular users (0–2 days per week); 78 were regular users (3–5 days per week); and 62 were daily users (6–7 days per week). Table 3.8 presents the percentage of users in each of these categories who have committed

Table 3.8
Percentage of Respondents with Non-Drug Crime

	Heroin User Group		
Average Non-drug Crime Type	Irregular	Regular	Daily
Any non-drug crime	87	94	97
Robbery	20	23	44
Burglary	31	42	56
Shoplifting (resale)	51	62	68
Other larcenies	36	53	60
Forgery	10	9	13
Con games	26	27	34
Prostitution	20	19	13
Pimping	10	6	6
Other illegal acts	38	40	42
Shoplifting (own use)*	31	35	32

*Shoplifting for own use is not included in any non-drug crime total.

Source: Adapted from Table B-6 in Bruce D. Johnson et al. (1985), *Taking Care of Business* (Lexington, Mass.: Lexington Books: 229).

various non-drug crimes. The type of non-drug crime that was committed by most addicts was shoplifting for resale purposes. Overall, 60 percent of the addicts admitted shoplifting for resale purposes and 33 percent reported shoplifting items for their own use. The percentage of addicts who shoplifted for resale purposes increased as the use of heroin increased to daily levels. A fuller and more detailed presentation of these addicts' criminal activity is found in Table 3.9. The statistics are derived from only those addicts who reported involvement in each of the crimes identified in the table. The daily users of heroin who shoplifted for resale reported an average of 106 incidents in the last year. Daily users who shoplifted for personal use reported an average of 17 incidents in the last year. Correspondingly, daily users realized an annual income of $3,341 from items shoplifted for resale but only $197 from items shoplifted for personal use (Johnson et al., 1985). Drug business enterprises stood out as the most frequently utilized and most lucrative type of criminal activity for all types of addicts. While there were extensive involvements in other types of non-drug crimes, it is clear that shoplifting is a frequently utilized mode of enhancing the budgets of these street addicts. The daily users, particularly when contrasted to the irregular

Table 3.9
Annualized Crime Rate Per Person Committing That Crime, Mean Lambdas*

| | Annualized Crime Rate per Person Committing That Crime | | |
| | Heroin User Group | | |
Type of Activity	Irregular	Regular	Daily
Non-drug crime*	133	174	215
Robbery	12	18	27
Burglary	14	36	60
Shoplifting (resale)	68	75	106
Other larcenies	16	41	33
Forgery	10	13	19
Con games	137	132	91
Prostitution	117	140	249
Pimping	19	35	23
Other illegal acts	19	30	16
Drug business crimes	276	931	1,029
Miscellaneous drug crimes	97	177	283
Minor crimes	116	77	109
Shoplifting (own use)	21	20	17
Fare evasion	127	95	132

*For a specific offense class (e.g., burglary), the mean lambda is the number of crimes by persons who committed one or more such crimes (i.e., are burglars). Persons who commit other crimes, but not this offense (burglary), are excluded from the denominator.

Source: Adapted from Table B-13 in Bruce D. Johnson et al. (1985), *Taking Care of Business* (Lexington, Mass.: Lexington Books: 236).

users, were much more involved in both drug and non-drug criminal activity.

Thus, the studies by Inciardi and Johnson et al. present unique and detailed data documenting the pervasive involvement of street addicts in shoplifting. Both studies refer to the propensity of addicts to gravitate toward less confrontive types of crime like shoplifting and away from higher risk crimes like robbery. They also refer to the addicts' inability to function in more complex and lucrative types of criminal activity such as gambling operations (recall Manny's problems in Chapter 2) or the higher levels of the illicit drug trade.

Finally, Kowalski and Faupel (1990) report on their field research on 768 heroin addicts from three major metropolitan area (563 male and 205 female; 34% white, 33% black, and 32% Hispanic). Looking at the

Table 3.10
Main Hustle Crimes of 768 Regular-Active Heroin Users by Sex

Main Hustle	Percentage of sample	Percentage of total crimes (median)	Total number of main hustle crimes (median)	Total number of crime types (median)
		Males (N=563)		
Drug Sale	71.9 (405)	69.0	150	4.0
Vice Crimes	2.8 (16)	64.6	175	4.0
Robbery	2.5 (14)	7.8	25	3.5
Burglary	5.5 (31)	68.0	100	4.0
Shoplifting	6.0 (34)	50.4	110	5.0
Stolen Goods	3.9 (22)	45.8	27	6.0
Auto Theft	4.4 (25)	64.5	200	5.0
Con Games	1.1 (6)	64.2	100	2.0
Other Theft	0.2 (1)	76.2	80	2.0
		Females (N=205)		
Drug Sale	27.8 (57)	72.6	150	4.0
Vice Crimes	56.6 (116)	69.2	230	4.0
Burglary	0.5 (1)	98.5	200	2.0
Shoplifting	9.8 (20)	61.1	100	4.0
Stolen Goods	0.5 (1)	44.4	100	4.0
Bad Paper	3.4 (7)	66.7	50	3.0
Pickpocketing	0.5 (1)	100.0	50	1.0
Other Theft	1.0 (2)	63.3	405	6.0

Source: Gregory S. Kowalski and Charles E. Faupel (1990), "Heroin Use, Crime, and the 'Main Hustle' " (Deviant Behavior 11(1): 9).

drugs and crime issue differently from the other two studies, they introduce the concept of the "main hustle" to refer to the crime specialization of a research subject. They operationalize this as the crime most frequently committed in the last year. Table 3.10 presents their data on the main hustle crime patterns (e.g., shoplifting committed by individuals without shoplifting as their main hustle was not presented in this study). For male addicts, drug sale activity (71.9%) was overwhelmingly identified as the main hustle and shoplifting (6%) was ranked second.

For the female addicts, vice crimes (56.6%) were the most frequent type of main hustle. This was followed by drug sales (27.8%) and shoplifting (9.8%). In an earlier pilot study, Charles Faupel (1986) reported that 36.7 percent of the female addicts and 18.8 percent of the male addicts "favored" shoplifting as their main hustle. Table 3.10 also shows that female addicts were more likely (61.1%) than males (50.4%) to concentrate on shoplifting. Both of these male and female addicts committed about the same number of shoplifting crimes and reported a similar number of involvements in other types of crime. Therefore, this study confirms that there was considerable crime specialization among street addicts and that they also committed a patterned variety of other kinds of offenses.

All these studies target the predominantly minority underclass segment of society, and most focus on street drug addicts.[6] They confirm that there is an inordinate amount of shoplifting done by these individuals. It is somewhat surprising that studies of the homeless, street kids, bag ladies, and so forth rarely mention shoplifting (e.g., Burt and Cohen, 1989) even though merchants often view them with a high level of suspicion. One exception is the research on criminality and homeless men by David Snow et al. (1989). Snow and his colleagues compared the police records of a random sample of homeless men with those of males from the general population of a large southwestern city. The rate of arrest was significantly higher for the homeless. This was mainly due to higher arrests for public intoxication and theft/shoplifting.

The only other study to investigate the relationship between homelessness and shoplifting is the innovative research conducted by Bill McCarthy and John Hagan (1991). They resourcefully collected self-report data from 396 homeless Toronto youth (under age 20) and 563 youth who were in school and living with their parents. In a companion article (forthcoming), the same authors argue that most self-report delinquency studies are flawed because they do *not* include out-of-school (homeless) youth. By excluding this sizable and potentially crucial segment of the population, previous self-report studies may have distorted our understanding of delinquency.[7] To rectify this typical sampling bias, McCarthy and Hagan focused their research on homeless youth. They discovered that homeless youth were involved in a wide variety of illegal acts and that their illegal involvements increased *after* leaving home. Shoplifting items valued at less than $50, for example, was reported by 42 percent of the youth while living at home and by 53 percent after leaving home. There was a smaller but still statistically significant increase in shoplifting items valued over $50 from 23 percent to 30 percent after leaving home. A larger increase in shoplifting after leaving home was noted for the homeless females and for youth who were deemed to be lower delinquency risks prior to their leaving home. Finally, youth who had been on the streets for more than a year were more involved in illegal behavior. The authors speculate that the increases in illegal behavior (and shoplifting) were attributed to the criminogenic conditions (economic destitution, contact with deviant peers, weakened social controls, and labeling experiences) that the youths encountered while on the streets. More of this type of research needs to be done so that we can refine our understanding of crime among the various types of street people.

OVERVIEW

This chapter has reviewed the extant research on demographic variables and shoplifting patterns. A tentative and sometimes crude profile of the kinds of people who are more likely to be involved was derived from this base of quantitative research. For example, there was a strong inverse relationship between age and shoplifting activity. Contrary to a popular stereotype, males were generally found to have higher rates of shoplifting activity than females. The limited research on race and ethnic variations in shoplifting suggests that only minor differences are evident in the population at large. The similarly scanty research on socioeconomic variables typically revealed slight to moderate inverse relationships between social class and shoplifting behavior. Research on heroin street addicts and initial research on homeless adults and youth revealed high rates of shoplifting.

These descriptive leads provide interesting and useful starting points for the analysis of shoplifting. There is also ample room for more and better quantitative research to develop even more precise descriptions of who shoplifts.

NOTES

1. More specific data on the exact age of these apprehended shoplifters show that the largest number of apprehensions were made on 14-year-old youth. Thirteen-year-old youth were the next most apprehended, and they were followed by 15-year-old youth.

2. A self-report study of nine middle and high schools by Dena Cox et al. (1990) found that shoplifting activity peaked slightly later. More sophomore students reported shoplifting in the last year, when they would have been freshmen (or about 14 years old).

3. Consider, for example, the following magazine articles: in *Mademoiselle*, "Shoplifting: Why Women Who Have Everything Steal" (Kopecky, 1980); in *Ladies Home Journal*, "Shoplifting: When "Honest" Women Steal" (Taylor, 1982); in *Cosmopolitan*, "Women Who Steal" (Brenton, 1985); and in *Mademoiselle*, "Excuse Me, Miss! Did You Pay for This?" (Bernikow, 1988).

4. There may be some basis for the belief that tourists are more likely to shoplift, as many of my respondents mention that they usually go outside their neighborhood or community to shoplift.

5. Robert Prus and Styllianoss Irini (1980) provide another insightful analysis of the hustles utilized by hookers and rounders who frequent slum bars and strip joints.

6. It would be very useful to have the same types of research on offenses committed by higher socioeconomic class addicts. This would help clarify the role that social class plays in the lives of individuals who are involved in various drug scenes.

7. Like the *Monitoring the Future* study and the research by Klemke (1982a), which were mentioned earlier.

4

TYPOLOGIES OF SHOPLIFTERS AND SHOPLIFTING

There is consensus now that there are many different types of delinquency, each with its own particular set of causal factors as well as its
own distinctive cluster of characteristics. Criminologists are generally
agreed that it is a mistake to treat the problem as if all delinquents were
alike.

Ruth Shonle Cavan and Theodore N. Ferdinand,
Juvenile Delinquency (p. 141)

By now the reader should be keenly aware that developing an understanding of shoplifters and shoplifting is not easy. The task is particularly
challenging because of the many dimensions and complex forms that
the phenomenon assumes. To reduce this complexity to a manageable
level, researchers have developed a variety of ways of classifying types
of shoplifting behavior or shoplifters. An assessment of the feasibility
and value of developing typologies of offenders has been made by Don
Gibbons (1985). He comes to the pessimistic conclusion that discovering
a precise classification scheme is not a very feasible goal. The key ob-
stacles are the complex dynamics and the tremendous diversity exhibited
by many deviants. He does acknowledge that developing typologies is
still justifiable for their heuristic value, in that they may stimulate researchers and theorists to pursue new leads. One classification scheme
may lead to one set of valuable insights, while another scheme may
contribute to our understanding in different ways. It is with this rationale
that a series of typologies can be explored for the ways they can facilitate
our understanding of shoplifting behavior and shoplifters.

EXPLORING TYPOLOGIES OF SHOPLIFTERS
AND SHOPLIFTING

Shoplifters can be distinguished from one another in many different ways. In the last chapter, demographic variables were found to be useful in specifying shoplifting patterns. Many researchers have made comparisons between male and female shoplifters; young, middle-aged, and elderly shoplifters; and lower class versus more affluent shoplifters. Gregory Schlueter et al. (1989) attempt to distinguish between rational and non-rational shoplifters. Others have identified shoplifters according to the types of items they usually steal. In earlier material, references were made to individuals who specialized in cigarettes, furs, meats, and handbags. Analysts have also examined shoplifters according to their modus operandi. Shoplifters range from those who crudely snatch items near an exit and run, to those contriving extensive con jobs like Manny and his partner (see Chapter 2) to those who shoplift only with the assistance of an insider (store employee). Some shoplifters operate only with the help of a partner(s), and others always shoplift alone. A small number of shoplifters have been known to utilize disguises (e.g., clothes that make them look like clergy or store personnel), but most simply attempt to look like typical shoppers.

Many typologies attempt to identify types of individuals who pose a higher risk of shoplifting. Philip Purpura (1984), for example, singles out juveniles/students, housewives, drunks/vagrants, addicts, "easy access" individuals (repairmen and delivery people serving the store), kleptomaniacs, and amateur and professional shoplifters as the main types that security personnel should be concerned about. John MacDonald (1980) narrows the categories down to amateurs, juveniles, narcotics addicts, professionals, and compulsive shoplifters. These examples indicate the range of categories scholars have proposed for shoplifting and shoplifters. Several of the more significant and powerful typologies will now be described.

BECKER'S TYPOLOGY OF DEVIANT BEHAVIOR

Drawing from the sociology of deviance literature, an elementary but useful typology has been developed by Howard Becker (1963). It can easily be adapted to shoplifting. Becker distinguishes between (1) an individual's behavior (if one has committed rule-breaking behavior or not), and (2) how others perceive and publicly label that behavior (as deviant or non-deviant). In developing his ideas, he articulates one of the early and important statements of what has been called the labeling perspective. Table 4.1 shows the four types that emerge when Becker's two dimensions are cross-classified. Becker's original terminology for

Table 4.1
Becker's Typology of Deviant Behavior

	Shoplifting Behavior	
	Yes	No
Labeled a Shoplifter		
Yes	Pure Shoplifter	Falsely Accused Shoplifter
No	Secret Shoplifter	Pure Non-shoplifter

Source: Adapted from Howard S. Becker (1963), *Outsiders: Studies in the Sociology of Deviance* (New York: The Free Press of Glencoe: 20).

these types has been changed to directly focus on shoplifting. As shown in Table 4.1, individuals who have shoplifted and have been detected-labeled as shoplifters are identified as *pure shoplifters*. They are contrasted with the *pure non-shoplifters*, individuals who have not shoplifted and who have not been labeled as shoplifters. The more interesting types, however, are the *secret shoplifters*, those who have shoplifted but not been labeled as such, and the *falsely accused shoplifters*, those who have not shoplifted but still have been labeled as shoplifters.

The four types encompass the logical possibilities that emerge from Becker's typology. However, as Gibbons (1985) has pointed out, reality presents a bewildering array of possibilities and numerous ambiguities. This makes it difficult to place some individuals into one cell of the typology. For example, is an individual who "really forgot" to pay for an item and is apprehended by security personnel a pure shoplifter or a falsely accused shoplifter? Whose definition of the situation, the accuser's or the accused's, should prevail?

The problematic enterprise of detecting and substantiating the existence of shoplifting poses a constant daily challenge to store security personnel. Numerous examples of legal proceedings of contested cases have been collected in *Selected Cases on the Law of Shoplifting* (Fein and Maskell, 1975). In many of these incidents the apprehended suspect claimed that he or she had been falsely accused.[1] This work highlights the extreme difficulty that security personnel continually face when making decisions about shoplifters.[2] Social scientists studying shoplifting are often confronted with similar problematic decisions.

For example, Becker's typology becomes difficult to use because an individual's behavior and how others label that behavior is constantly changing. This means that an individual could fit into each one of the cells at different times of a single day and certainly at different points in one's life. Research to capture this dynamic, every-changing reality is beyond contemporary social science capabilities. Klemke's study (1982a) of high school students, however, provided percentages on how many—at least at *this point in their lives*—could be placed into three of the four cells identified by Becker. The students' self-reports of shoplifting behavior and apprehensions for shoplifting by store personnel revealed that 15 percent of the high school students were *pure shoplifters* (had shoplifted and been apprehended), 48 percent were *secret shoplifters* (had shoplifted but never been apprehended), and 37 percent were *pure non-shoplifters* (had not shoplifted or been accused of it). Respondents were not asked if they had ever been unfairly accused of shoplifting.

This finding, that more individuals were involved in deviant behavior than were apprehended, is consistent with other self-report studies (e.g., Erickson and Empey, 1963). Even so, Klemke's data exaggerate the likelihood of being apprehended for specific acts of shoplifting because the percentage is not calculated for the number of times one has been apprehended for the number of times one has shoplifted. One of the few studies to do this is Inciardi's (1980) study of 149 female heroin addicts. He found that only 47 apprehensions (0.5%) occurred out of the 8,713 shoplifting acts committed by his respondents. This confirms the existence of vast amounts of "secret" shoplifting and the importance of this cell in Becker's typology. Because only a few of the many shoplifting acts are detected and result in an apprehension, this fact again raises questions about the accuracy of research based on store apprehension records.

CAMERON'S TYPOLOGY OF SHOPLIFTERS

The most popular typology of shoplifters has been presented by Mary Owen Cameron (1964). She borrows slang terms from the thieves' argot of her time to distinguish between two main types of shoplifters. These are the "boosters," who are professional shoplifters, and the "snitches," who are amateur shoplifters. The most important difference is that boosters steal merchandise to sell, whereas snitches steal merchandise for their own use. Boosters are further divided into "heels," who specialize in shoplifting, and "ordinary" boosters, who engage in shoplifting as just one of their many forms of illicit activity. The latter are frequently involved in prostitution, narcotics addiction, and alcoholism, and they shoplift to support their habits.

Snitches are described by Cameron as chronic, premeditative shoplifters. They typically are not involved in criminal subcultures and do not have prior criminal arrests. Usually, they steal items of small monetary value and appear to be respectable people. According to Cameron (1964), about 10 percent of department store shoplifters are boosters and the other 90 percent are snitches. While the term "boosters" is still widely used today, the terms "snitch," "heel," and "ordinary" booster seem to have lost much of their popularity.

This typology has a great deal of initial appeal even though it does not exhibit a tight logical structure or rest on a very strong empirical base. Closer and more serious scrutiny, however, reveals that it may not be as useful as it appears. More recent research by Johnson et al. (1985) shows that significant numbers of boosters who shoplift for resale also shoplift for their own use (see Tables 3.8 and 3.9). Likewise, the view that snitches are chronic shoplifters can also be challenged by recent research (see Table 3.3) showing that many young people are only infrequently involved in shoplifting.

A final concern about Cameron's typology is her assertion that snitches are premeditative thieves. Unfortunately, very little systematic evidence is available on this issue. Research by Moore (1984) characterized 15.4 percent of a sample of *convicted* shoplifters as impulse shoplifters. Certainly, this percentage would be considerably larger in a random sample of shoplifters. There is also some evidence, found in Katz's (1988) accounts of shoplifting by college students, that emphasizes the powerful spur-of-the-moment attractions stimulated by store merchandise that can trigger shoplifting incidents. Booster Box 5 contains two illustrative examples from Katz's research.

Booster Box 5
MERCHANDISE STIMULATING SHOPPING IMPULSES

Example A: There we were, in the most lucrative department Mervyn's had to offer two curious (but very mature) adolescent girls: the cosmetic and jewelry department.... We didn't enter the store planning to steal anything. In fact, I believe we had "given it up" a few weeks earlier; but once my eyes caught sight of the beautiful white and blue necklaces alongside the counter, a spark inside me was once again ignited.... Those exquisite puka necklaces were calling out to me, "Take me! Wear me! I can be yours!" All I needed to do was take them to make it a reality.

Example B: A gold-plated compact that I had seen on a countertop kept playing on my mind. Heaven knows I didn't need it, and at $40 it was obviously overpriced. Still, there was something about the design that intrigued me. I went back to the counter and picked up the compact again. At that moment, I felt an overwhelming urge.

Source: Jack Katz. 1988. *Seductions of Crime: Moral and Sensual Attractions in Doing Evil*. New York: Basic Books: 54–55.

Many of the respondents I interviewed for this book also emphasized that their shoplifting was often a spur-of-the-moment act. One, for example, stated that "I never went into a store knowing that I was going to shoplift. I would just be walking around and then take something, makeup or candy, never thinking before that I would. Just see it, walk by, and take it. Didn't really think about it." Likewise, 56 percent of the respondents in my convenience sample of college student shoplifters claimed that they had not planned on shoplifting prior to entering the store. Even Cameron hedges on this issue and hints that "There may or may not exist in any considerable number a third group of shoplifters consisting of impulsive persons who are overcome by an unpremeditated desire for a particular object" (Cameron, 1964: 146). The evidence, therefore, suggests that impulse shoplifters should be incorporated into any comprehensive typology of shoplifters.

MOORE'S TYPOLOGY OF SHOPLIFTERS

The only effort to develop a typology of shoplifting behavior from empirical evidence is Richard Moore's (1984) research. His study was conducted in a medium-sized community (175,000) that had just initiated a new statute making shoplifting a municipal offense. Moore's subjects were the first 300 convicted shoplifters referred to the probation department for pre-sentence investigations. Each offender completed a questionnaire, was interviewed by a probation counselor, and was subjected to a psychological evaluation (to assess personality characteristics and intellectual functioning). Information was obtained on their (1) frequency of shoplifting; (2) primary precipitating factor(s); (3) attitude toward shoplifting as a crime; (4) use of stolen goods; and (5) reaction to detection, prosecution, and conviction. Based on this accumulated information, Moore derived five types of shoplifters.

Nutshell summaries of these types are described as follows. The *impulse shoplifters* had limited shoplifting activity, often only once or twice. They had not planned their thefts and were often stimulated to take inexpensive but tempting items. When stopped by security personnel, they often claimed to be in a daze and shocked to find that they had an unpaid-for item in their possession. They typically exhibited high levels of guilt, shame, and embarrassment about their behavior. Moore identified 15.4 percent of the sample as impulse shoplifters. The *occasional shoplifters* reported having taken items three to ten times during the last year. Financial reasons seemed to be secondary to doing a challenging act or complying with peer pressures. When apprehended, they acknowledged their guilt but minimized the seriousness of the act. Fifteen percent of his sample were deemed occasional shoplifters by Moore.

The third type were the *episodic shoplifters*. These individuals went through periodic episodes of shoplifting and exhibited severe emotional and psychological problems (several examples from Moore's work were presented in Chapter 2). Despite holding attitudes that shoplifting was wrong, they were likely to continue their pattern of shoplifting until they received professional therapy. They were usually compliant when apprehended. Only 1.7 percent of Moore's subjects fit this pattern. The largest category, *amateur shoplifters*, encompassed 56.4 percent of those studied. These individuals had developed a regular (often weekly) pattern of shoplifting. Having been successful in the past, they found this to be an economically rewarding activity (each averaged $700 annually). They made conscious decisions to steal and were aware of its illegality. When apprehended, they usually attempted to claim only minimal involvement in prior shoplifting activity.

Finally, the remaining 11.7 percent of the subjects were identified as *semi-professional shoplifters*. Shoplifting had become part of their life-style. They shoplifted frequently (at least once a week and averaged about $1,250 annually) and utilized more skilled techniques and precautions than the other types of shoplifters. They also took more luxury and expensive items and were the only type to report doing modest amounts of shoplifting for resale purposes. Many of these shoplifters did not perceive shoplifting to be legally or morally wrong because "everybody steals" or "stores are ripping us off." Frequently they were experiencing frustrations in their daily lives. When apprehended, they were likely to pour out a "prepared story" in an effort to talk their way out of legal consequences. If this did not work, they were likely to become very angry and claim that they were being treated unfairly.

Moore's typology represents an ambitious effort to incorporate five potentially important dimensions into one typology. One gets the feeling, however, that too much was attempted. Unfortunately, Moore does not report the standards that were utilized to categorize individuals. The impression is that many compromises were required in order to squeeze individuals into one of the five types. There is also a question about the validity of information elicited from individuals being interviewed by their probation officer. Clearly, a more neutral interviewer would have increased the credibility of the data. It should also be noted that Moore is not studying a random sample of shoplifters. Instead, his sample is *convicted* shoplifters. The large percentage (69.8%) who were frequent shoplifters (episodic, amateur, or semi-professionals) is, therefore, much larger than would be the case for a random sample of shoplifters. This is because stores are much more likely to prosecute shoplifters who seem to be serious offenders. It also appears that Moore's finely-tuned distinctions between the impulse and the occasional shoplifter may be too slight to maintain. Finally, the medium-sized community base may have minimized the percentage of certain types of shoplifters, such as the semi-professionals. It may also have some impact on Moore's not making any note of shoplifters from the heroin street addict subculture. Despite these problems and limitations, Moore does provide a unique analysis and a point of comparison for future research.

LEMERT'S TYPOLOGY OF DEVIANT BEHAVIOR

Another basic typology has been developed by Edwin Lemert (1951). His general classification of types of deviation is based on answers to the question: What is the main cause of the deviation? His simple but powerful response points to elementary yet important distinctions. He identifies three varieties of deviance causation. They are (1) individual deviation; (2) situational deviation; and (3) systematic deviation. These types can be easily applied to shoplifting behavior. In fact, Lemert presents several examples of shoplifting in his discussion on crime. The *individual deviation*, for example, is deviance that emanates from "within the skin" of the individual. It may spring from hereditary, physiological, or psychological conditions. The classic, but rare, example of the individual deviation type of shoplifter would be the kleptomaniac. Likewise, Moore's episodic shoplifters fall into this type. Physiological explanations of shoplifting have enjoyed several waves of popularity (recall the linkage of female sexual disorders to shoplifting during the late 1800s described in Chapter 2). A few apprehended shoplifters do have physical and psychological conditions that are being treated with psychotrophic drugs. Several investigators acknowledge that claims by apprehended shoplifters that recent medication had put them into a "dazed" or "zombie-like" condition may be valid (Arboleda-Florez, Durie, and Costello, 1977; Williams and Dalby, 1986). Many other contemporary writers still stress the importance of psychological explanations of shoplifting (these will be developed in the next chapter).

Lemert's second type, the *situational deviation*, moves into the sociological domain. Sounding like the early sociological theorist Emile Durkheim (1951), Lemert attributes this type of deviance to compelling external forces that could push an ordinarily law-abiding individual into deviance. Both *temporary crises* and *chronic conditions* are cited by Lemert as crime-producing situations. A wide variety of external stresses and strains can overwhelm an individual and result in deviance. Anthony

Mawson (1987) develops a similar model whereby temporary stress is linked to what he calls *transient* criminality.

Several examples illustrate the temporary crisis type of deviance. One would be when a recently laid-off worker resorts to shoplifting food to feed his/her hungry family. Another classic example was provided by one of my own respondents. She reported how, as a very "straight" 13-year-old, she had been raped. Not knowing how to deal with the trauma and embarrassment that overwhelmed her, she went "on the run" to a nearby metropolitan area. Not having any financial resources or support system, she relied on shoplifting to supply her subsistence needs for several days. Being an inept novice shoplifter, she was soon apprehended by a store security person. Thus, a "normal" person thrust into a crisis situation responded by committing a series of atypical behaviors.[3] In the next chapter, the neutralization theoretical perspective will be related to Lemert's crisis type of deviance. The immediate situational determinants of crime will also be explored from the rational choice theoretical perspective.

In addition to temporary crisis situations, Lemert focuses on longer lasting criminogenic conditions that lead to chronic situational deviance. Traditional sociological perspectives and concepts are used to illustrate this type of causation pattern. For example, he refers to anomie, culture conflict, stresses confronting adolescents, and the tension-inducing characteristics of American culture (individualism, competitiveness, and breakdown of social control) to explain our high rates of crime. Specifically addressing shoplifting, he states that:

While shoplifting occasionally may be symptomatic compulsive behavior or bear the imprint of professional grifting, much of it is situational, related to low wages coupled with high prices and to the exposure of an abundance of coveted goods in a mass situation where policing is difficult to maintain efficiently." (Lemert, 1951: 297)

This quote insightfully identifies the chronic situational pressures and socioeconomic context that may stimulate shoplifting behavior. In the following chapter, anomie and social control theories will be developed as explanations fitting Lemert's chronic situational deviance.

Finally, Lemert describes *systematic deviation*. This is deviance that is stimulated and supported by a deviant group or subculture. When an individual is a member of a deviant group, it is not difficult to explain or understand why that person commits deviant acts. If, for example, one's parents, friends, or colleagues are encouraging, rewarding, and committing crimes, then one is likely to conform to their deviant norms. Numerous examples of groups and subcultures that have developed shoplifting norms (ranging from informal groups of adolescent friends or drug addicts to more professionalized troupes) were presented in Chapters 2 and 3. In the following chapter, the socialization theoretical perspective will be developed as the main explanation of Lemert's systematic deviance.

Lemert's typology is more than a simple sorting out of major causes of deviance. The additional complexity arises from his recognition that every deviant act is, to some degree, stimulated by various combinations of individual, situational, and systematic factors. While one of these sources of deviance may be the most important factor in a particular case, all may be operating to some degree. In some cases, it may be difficult to specify which factor is most important. For example, a person who recently began shoplifting may have an emotionally unstable personality (individual factor); may have experienced a recent economic crisis (situational factor); and may have developed several close friends who are boosters (systematic factor). One can also hypothesize that this type of person may be more likely to end up shoplifting than an individual for whom only one or two of these factors are operating.

Likewise, Lemert's typology can be utilized to capture the dynamics of social reality in tracing how causes of shoplifting behavior change over time. Thus, an individual's initial involvement in shoplifting may be due to a situational crisis (e.g., being raped). But as one goes on the run, gets arrested, spends time in a detention facility, and develops deviant friends, one may quickly become a systematic deviant.

COMPARING AND SYNTHESIZING SEVERAL TYPOLOGIES

Each of the typologies that have been discussed has its strengths and limitations. It is instructive to see how they overlap with each other. Table 4.2 shows the similarities and connections between the typologies developed by Cameron, Moore, and Lemert. As can be seen, the Cameron and Moore typologies are quite similar to each other. The major difference is that Cameron does not include an equivalent to Moore's episodic type. Even though they use slightly different terminology and category breakdowns, there seems to be a considerable amount of similarity between their types.

Table 4.2 also shows how Lemert's types relate to the other types. Furthermore, extending his reasoning leads to different hypothesized patterns of causation for different types of shoplifter. For example, the most important causal order pattern for semi-professional shoplifters should be systematic factors, followed by chronic situational and then individual factors. The causal pattern for amateur shoplifters should be chronic situational factors followed by systematic and individual factors. Temporary situational factors are likely to be most important for occasional and impulse shoplifters. At the other extreme, episodic shoplifters

Table 4.2
Similarities and Connections between Various Shoplifting Typologies

Cameron's Typology	Moore's Typology	Lemert's Typology: (Expected Order of Importance of Casual Factors)
Boosters		Systematic
Heel		
	Semi-Professional	(Systematic, Chronic Situational, Individual)
Ordinary		
Snitches		Situational
Chronic	Amateur	(Chronic Situational, Systematic, Individual)
	Occasional	
Impulse		(Temporary Situational, Systematic, Individual)
	Impulse	
		Individual
	Episodic	(Individual, Crisis Situational, Systematic)

are more likely to be influenced by individual factors followed by crisis situational and systematic factors. At the present time, only anecdotal evidence verifies the existence of these hypothesized patterns.

SHOPLIFTERS: PATHOLOGICAL DEVIANTS, SOCIETAL VICTIMS, OR FRUGAL CUSTOMERS?

Before leaving this section, it is appropriate to make one final point of comparison in how various analysts have formulated very different conceptions of the shoplifter. Most researchers seem to begin with the assumption that shoplifters are abnormal or deviant. As will be developed in the next chapter, psychiatric/psychological analysts are especially prone to detect psychopathological conditions in most shoplifters. Sociologists have often viewed shoplifting as a response to criminogenic social conditions or societal victimization. In either case, shoplifting occurs because something (psychological or social) has gone "out of kilter."

In a contrasting and appealing conception, the shoplifter can be viewed as a consummate frugal customer. Here the shoplifter is viewed as a basically normal individual who periodically stretches the boundaries of proper customer behavior. In a consumption-driven society we should not be surprised or shocked at individuals maximizing their "purchasing productivity." As Robert Kraut claims, the motivation for shoplifting "is the same as for normal shopping: the acquisition of goods at minimum cost" (1976: 365). Many investigators have noted that the peaks of shoplifting activity typically coincide with the peaks of legitimate shopping (late afternoons, weekends, and during sales and at Christmas time).[5] Research universally shows that most shoplifters take items for their personal use.

Cameron (1964) often referred to the respectability of many shoplifters (snitches and, particularly, middle-class females) in contrast to viewing them as serious deviants. She also claimed that people often steal in the same way that they go about buying items. This is indirectly confirmed by contemporary consumer researchers. For example, several phenomenological analyses of normal shopping (Tauber, 1972), compulsive buying (O'Guinn and Faber, 1989), and impulse buying (Rook, 1987) sound very similar to Katz's (1988) phenomenological analysis of shoplifting. Moschis (1987) and Cox et al. (1990) also point to the similarity between shoplifting and normal consumer behavior.

The distinction between the shoplifter as a pathological person, societal victim, or frugal customer will be evident in many of the theoretical perspectives that are presented in the next chapter. Instead of presuming that only one of these views is correct, it is highly likely that some shoplifters fit the pathological conception, others are best seen as societal victims, and many others fit the frugal customer conception.

OVERVIEW

This chapter has presented several typologies that provide insightful ways of analyzing shoplifters and shoplifting behavior. Becker's typology distinguishes individuals who shoplift from those who do not. More important, it demands that researchers consider whether others label the individual as a shoplifter or not. His analysis also sensitizes us to consider the interesting categories of secret shoplifters and falsely accused shoplifters. The remaining typologies focus only on those who have actually shoplifted. Cameron and Moore, for example, both attempt to identify the main types of shoplifters. Cameron borrowed her booster-snitch distinctions from the thieves' subculture, while Moore derived his five types from research on convicted shoplifters. The Moore typology is more comprehensive, but clear guidelines need to be spelled out before other researchers can utilize it. As Gibbons (1985) forewarned, neither of these typologies stands as a precise or flawless way of classifying shoplifters. Instead, they should be viewed as primarily valuable as a stimulus and point of comparison for other analysts.

Finally, Lemert's typology and its rich variety of insights provides a good introduction to the study of a particular type of crime like shoplifting. It sensitizes us to the major sources of crime causation and how the causal factors may vary for different types of shoplifters. Another contrast highlighted how analysts have traditionally viewed shoplifters as pathological deviants or societal victims. It was suggested that it might also be appropriate to regard some shoplifters as frugal customers. More important, the introduction and discussion of these typologies paves the way for detailed examination of psychological (individual factors) and sociological (systematic and situational factors) theories that are discussed in the next chapter.

NOTES

1. For a general discussion of the issue of false accusations, see Klemke and Tiedeman (1981).

2. Recall the difficulties that were noted in the discussion of observational studies of shoplifting in Chapter 1.

3. Recall the finding of McCarthy and Hagan (1991) that homeless youth shoplifted more after they became street kids.

4. Stores may in fact foster the view that customers can take things without paying for them when they offer free samples (of food, perfumes, etc.). Likewise, dramatic price reductions (30% to 70%) and sales promotions of "two for the price of one," coupons, mail-in rebates, and the like may create customer attitudes that one is being ripped off if one pays the full price or that the store may not care if one takes little items.

5. This may mean that shoplifters are simply invoking their alternative mode of acquiring merchandise. Or they may be shoplifting during busy store times because they believe their chances of being detected are lower.

5

PSYCHIATRIC/PSYCHOLOGICAL AND SOCIOLOGICAL THEORIES OF SHOPLIFTING

As unattractive morally as crime may be, we must appreciate that there is *genuine experiential creativity* in it as well. We should then be able to see what are, for the subject, the authentic attractions of crime and we should be able to explain variations in criminality beyond what can be accounted for by background factors.

Jack Katz, *Seduction of Crime:*
Moral and Sensual Attractions in Doing Evil (p. 8)

A perceptive and powerful statement has been succinctly crafted by Clyde Kluckholm and Henry Murray: "Every man is in certain respects (a) like all other men, (b) like some other men, and (c) like no other man" (1944: 53). Pharaphrasing Kluckholm's statement to fit the topic at hand, one can say the following: Every shoplifter is in certain respects (a) like all other shoplifters, (b) like some other shoplifters, and (c) like no other shoplifter. This simple statement acknowledges the similarities and diversity within the phenomenon of shoplifting. Furthermore, as George Herbert Mead (1934) has advocated, there are complex dynamics between the individual (shoplifter) as a *product* of social reality and as a *creator* of social reality that continue to tease and tantalize sociologists. While sociocultural factors that increase the likelihood of shoplifting will be emphasized in this chapter, the role that the individual plays in this process (as recommended in the extract from Jack Katz that opens this chapter) is also integrated into the analysis.

Because understanding shoplifting behavior is a major goal, much of the data comes from the individual's own perspective. This is a logical first step; it is also expedient because most existing research on shop-

lifting focuses on individuals. Early and current psychiatric/psycholog-
ical and sociological theories applicable to shoplifting will be reviewed
here. Qualitative and quantitative research evidence will be analyzed to
assess the value of these theories. While a more rigorous and definitive
test of the theories—or better yet, the development of a theory of shoplifting—might be desired, it is not feasible given the present state of
knowledge. Instead, it seems more productive to explore how the rich
tradition of deviance theories is useful in understanding shoplifting behavior. It will be the main task of this chapter.

PSYCHIATRIC/PSYCHOLOGICAL THEORIES OF
SHOPLIFTING—PAST AND PRESENT

Because systematic studies of large random samples of shoplifters are
rare, explanations of shoplifting have often been constructed from resourceful and imaginative analyses of a few interesting cases. Frequently, factors within the person (Lemert's "individual" deviance) have
been identified as the source of shoplifting behavior. As I pointed out
in Chapter 2, early medical professionals often blamed shoplifting on a
variety of pathological physical sexual conditions. Before long, psychiatrists imposed their interpretation that shoplifting was caused by various psychological pathologies (Abelson, 1989a, 1989b; O'Brien, 1983).

The Freudian psychoanalytic perspective was an integral part of many
early studies of shoplifters and continues to influence contemporary
discussions. An example of the approach is vividly illustrated in the case
of Sigrid. This woman had an extensive background of thievery and
shoplifting. Her neurotic personality was studied and treated by Franz
Alexander and William Healy (1935). Booster Box 6 summarizes the
lengthy analysis of material obtained from 120 therapy sessions with
her.

BOOSTER BOX 6
SIGRID, THE UNDETECTED SHOPLIFTER

The objects stolen by Sigrid covered a wide range of articles.
They consisted of all sorts of clothing and jewelry, but she has
also taken other things for her own use. She also was inclined
to take items such as toys and practical items that she would
give away to a needy family that she had befriended. Several
times she has taken many articles, but felt so guilty that she
returned to the store and secretly returned the items. Sigrid was

particularly inclined to steal handbags and pocketbooks. She takes great pleasure in her large collection she has accumulated. The authors assert that her desire for these items is rooted in the symbolic meaning that they represent female genital organs to her and for their inside cleanliness.

The analysts assert that Sigrid does not know why or how come she is driven to steal. They conclude that it is evident to them that the stealing serves to release her tremendous sexual tensions because she describes the emotional excitement and relief that she experiences while stealing.

Alexander and Healy also feel that Sigrid's personality was affected by an Oedipus situation. Stealing supposedly allowed her relief from the guilt feelings that she had internalized for competing with her mother for her father.

Alexander and Healy summarize their findings as follows:

Sigrid's inferiority feelings have been overtly based on her early relationships, her unfortunate life situation, and the autoeroticism which she condemns. Unconsciously she feels that there is something wanting in the structure of her personality. This is made very plain in the analysis of her compulsion, which shows that her excessive stealing of clothes cannot be passed over lightly as merely indicating that the finery taken was for the purpose of making herself appear attractive or that she might exhibit her good taste in dress. The deeper picture is of her desire above all things to be another person, 'a new person,' successfully feminine. . . . Some of the stealing, however, represents the wish to be a man, but not the woman she is. Or perhaps the unconscious wish is to be a woman and at the same time to have a penis. In any case the stealing seems to have a bisexual determination: Sigrid is not altogether content to be only a man or a woman. She wants to be both.

Source: Franz Alexander and William Healy. 1935. *Roots of Crime*. New York: Alfred A. Knopf:112; 115–16).

This case study illustrates a classic psychoanalytical analysis. The authors repeatedly emphasize the importance of child-parent relationships, unconscious motivations, and sexual themes as factors underlying Sigrid's stealing.[1] The approach and the reasoning may seem antiquated and perhaps even farfetched to many readers.

A contemporary psychoanalyst, Louise Kaplan (1991), presents numerous examples of the traditional psychoanalytical conception of kleptomania. She illustrates the Freudian interpretation with the case of Lillian, who stole silky garments that aroused her sexually (sexual fetish) and supposedly represented or compensated for her missing penis. While Kaplan retains a great deal of the Freudian perspective, her own explanation of shoplifting expands to incorporate how stealing also represents a "commodity fetish" that alienated contemporary citizens commit, hoping to alleviate their depression and anxieties.

Also in the psychiatric tradition, Fabian Rouke (1955) asserts, without providing supporting data, that about 10 percent of all shoplifters are professional thieves, 3 percent steal for material gain, and the remaining 87 percent steal because of emotional difficulty. His analysis focused on 65 apprehended shoplifters who had been referred to him for treatment. No details are given about how the subjects were selected, but one suspects that store or legal personnel had determined that they would benefit from psychological treatment. Rouke's analysis of these clients/subjects uncovered four primary psychological forces causing the shoplifting behavior. He found that shoplifting was due to (1) unfulfilled sexual gratification; (2) the need to gain status or social acceptance; (3) a desire to satisfy an unconscious need for humiliation and punishment; and (4) a desire to gain revenge against one's parents. He claims, again without documentation, that these four factors were about equally evident in his clients/subjects.

A more moderate example of the psychiatric perspective is found in W. Lindesay Neustatter's "The Psychology of Shoplifting" (1954). He analyzes five cases of middle-aged females who he acknowledges were sent to him because they were not typical shoplifters. After presenting an in-depth description of each case, he identifies the similarities between them and the potentially significant idiosyncratic features of each case. The generalizations are (1) that none of the cases were obsessive-compulsive (kleptomaniacs), experienced any sexual problem, or seemed to shoplift for financial gain; (2) that all of the subjects were experiencing tension and/or depression, particularly in their relationships with significant others; and (3) that at least three were very suggestible, having been diagnosed as hysterics. Hence, he concludes that when susceptible personality types experience stressful situation, they may be pushed into an atypical type of behavior like shoplifting.

Another analysis was conducted on 32 arrested shoplifters referred to a psychiatric facility for assessment (Arboleda-Florez, Durie, and Costello, 1977). Many of the individuals were experiencing financial, family, and/or medical problems at the time of the offense. The researchers did not find any cases that fit the kleptomania pattern.[2]

Psychological explanations remain popular today. Ann Appelbaum and Herbert Klemmer (1984), for example, divide the causes of shoplifting into sociological (primarily poverty and peer-stimulated shoplifting as a competitive sport) and psychological factors. The psychological causes are evident in individual shoplifters who (1) have poor impulse control; (2) are sociopathic; (3) are neurotic (i.e., have unconscious feelings of envy or hatred); or (4) exhibit other manifestations of severe mental disorders (e.g., drug, alcohol, or eating disorders). Only minimal research evidence is supplied by these authors. Anthony Mawson (1987) and H. V. Ziolko (1988) also point to cases where there appears to be a connection between anorexia nervosa and shoplifting activity.

While not explicitly focusing on shoplifting, several clinical psychologists (e.g., Witkins, 1988; Damon, 1988) focus on another type of "deviant" consumer behavior. Based on their clinical work, they describe many cases of individuals, primarily females, who are *addicted to shopping*. Their depiction of the "shopaholic" appears to be a revival of the kleptomaniac concept with a slightly different behavioral manifestation. The shopaholic is described as a troubled, angry, depressed, unloved person who seeks to escape his or her negative feelings and problems by embarking on uncontrollable shopping binges. While the writers do not mention shoplifting, it seems likely that the "out of control" shoppers might also resort to shoplifting to alleviate their psychological tensions. Both writers prescribe a formula (ranging from behavior modification strategies to shopaholic therapy groups) for overcoming compulsive shopping behavior.

Several psychologists have conducted quantitative research on samples of college students. They have attempted to ascertain whether college student shoplifters have more pathological personalities than non-shoplifting students (Beck and McIntyre, 1977; Moore, 1983). The Beck and McIntyre study, utilizing the Minnesota Multiphasic Personality Inventory as its central instrument, found that self-reported shoplifters scored significantly higher on the Psychopathic Deviate and Mania scales. This finding was challenged by Moore's study, which utilized the California Psychological Inventory. He did *not* find more maladjustment when apprehended shoplifters were compared to non-shoplifters. Both studies can be criticized for their methodology. Because they were based on small non-random samples, questions have been raised about their generalizability. It has also been claimed that the psychological tests that were used are flawed, because crucial subscales already contain items about criminal behavior (Gottfredson and Hirschi, 1990). This injects the possibility of a serious tautological error in which the *outcome* is seen as the *cause* of the behavior.

Moore conducted another study (1984) of 300 convicted shoplifters. These subjects were classified according to the American Psychiatric Association's Diagnostic and Statistical Manual procedures. He concluded that about 18 percent of the subjects were exhibiting some psychological pathology (i.e., substance abuse or mental or emotional problems). In only 1.7 percent of the cases, however, was mental illness considered to be primarily responsible for the shoplifting behavior (recall the examples of "episodic" shoplifters presented in Chapter 2). Other contemporary studies also conclude that psychological pathology is a significant factor in only a small percentage of shoplifters (Cameron, 1964; Gibbens, 1981; Yates, 1986).

In summary, it appears that the psychiatric/psychoanalytic stereotype of the shoplifter as a mentally disordered kleptomaniac has lost much of its efficacy (Edwards, 1970).[3] Attempts to impute unconscious and symbolic motives, particularly of a sexual nature, are less credible to most contemporary analysts. Some studies based on non-representative clinical samples still do uncover evidence of mental pathology (Cupchick and Atcheson, 1983). More recent studies, however, conclude that *most shoplifters are characterized by relatively normal psychological health and personalities that are indistinguishable from non-shoplifters.* This conclusion is reinforced in an insightful and searing critique of the scientific deficiencies present in most psychiatric attempts to explain crime (Hakeem, 1985).

Moderate psychological approaches seem to offer more potential insight about shoplifting. In fact, when psychologists explore how interpersonal relationships, socialization experiences, social reinforcement, and the like affect individuals, they often sound like sociologists. The next section explores how the major sociological theories of deviance-crime can enhance our understanding of shoplifting. At several points, contributions by psychologists will be incorporated where they supplement and complement the work being done by sociologists.

SOCIOLOGICAL THEORIES AND SHOPLIFTING

Sociologists have expended a great deal of energy seeking meaningful explanations of deviance-crime. Their theories provide explanations that account for the "situational" and "systematic" types of deviance identified by Lemert. Before developing these theories, it seems appropriate to make a distinction between theories that attempt to explain (1) *general motivations* toward deviance-criminality, and (2) those that seek to understand why a *particular type of crime* or *crime event* has been committed. Cullen (1984), Cornish and Clarke (1986), and Gottfredson and Hirschi (1990) have all persuasively argued that sorting out these levels of analysis helps to clarify the theoretical analysis of deviance. Generally, anomie-strain, social control, socialization, and labeling[4] theories fit the first level of analysis, while neutralization and rational choice theories fit the second. Cullen (1984) points out that most of the general theories also touch upon the second and more specific level of analysis. He advocates focusing much more attention on how generalized deviant motivations become structured into specific deviant acts like shoplifting.

Consistent with this goal, the following analysis will seek ways of connecting the general criminogenic conditions to the immediate situational and individual conditions that lead to shoplifting. As recommended by W. Bryan Groves and Michael Lynch (1990) and Robert Agnew (1990), there will also be a concerted effort to consider how well sociologists' theories match the information and explanations of shoplifting obtained from shoplifters. Interview excerpts and questionnaire data will be included to illustrate the strengths and limitations of particular theoretical perspectives. Because the research evidence is limited and often of marginal quality, this analysis provides more of a preliminary assessment than an attempt to attain theoretical closure.

ANOMIE-STRAIN THEORIES AND SHOPLIFTING

The first major sociological deviance theory focuses on how individuals fit into the economic structure of the society and seek to attain economic cultural goals. This is an appropriate starting point, as shoplifting is usually considered to be primarily an economic crime. The concept of anomie (a societal condition of normlessness) was initially formulated by Durkheim (1951) in 1897. Since then it has evolved as research and other theoretical ideas have been developed. Anomie-strain theory with an economic focus is especially indebted to the early work of Robert Merton (1938). In a classic paper he theorized that a great deal of deviance can be attributed to the importance American society places on becoming economically successful without always providing adequate access to the legitimate means to obtain this goal. This disjuncture was called a condition of anomie, which Merton theorized propelled frustrated individuals into various deviant modes of adaptation (innovation, ritualism, retreatism, and rebellion). Because *poor* people were more likely to face structural barriers to legitimate career opportunities (i.e., to experience anomie), they were more likely to experience frustration and become deviant. According to Merton, official crime statistics verified this pattern.

Over the years Merton's theory has stimulated much debate, research, and theoretical refinement, but rarely has it been applied to shoplifting. This is surprising, as shoplifting appears to be a classic example of Merton's *innovation* deviant mode of adaptation. Clearly, at a simple descriptive level, shoplifting can be viewed as one illegitimate means of obtaining culturally approved material items and symbols of economic success.

The following analysis explores the meaningfulness of Merton's anomie theory and/or variations of it for explaining shoplifting behavior. First, at the societal (structural or macro) level, does shoplifting follow the pattern predicted by Merton (higher rates of deviance in the lower class)? Second, at the personal (micro) level, how important are economic reasons as a motivation for shoplifting? While Merton was primarily concerned with societal level explanations, it seems reasonable to explore whether individual shoplifters articulate motivations that reflect his notion of anomie. In fact, most tests of Merton's ideas have utilized questionnaire and interview data (e.g., Short et al., 1965; Agnew, 1983; Elliott et al., 1985).

Unfortunately, very little systematic evidence is available to support the structural level of Merton's argument. Much of this is due to the paucity of high quality official shoplifting statistics for larger social units (cities, states, etc.). Even where they are available, one can have little confidence in the comparability of such statistics from one city or state to another. Several popular articles are related to Merton's structural thesis. For example, two journalistic reports, based on police statistics and interviews with security personnel, concluded that communities hit particularly hard by economic downswings (anomie) experienced significant increases in shoplifting (Paikert, 1982; Wiessler, 1982). Another interesting example is the "epidemic of shoplifting" that occurred when the Berlin Wall was opened. Reunification allowed a flood of economically deprived Eastern Europeans to shop (and shoplift) in West Berlin for items that were not available at home (Breslau, 1990).

Studies focusing on the relationship between social class and shoplifting were presented in Chapter 3 and will only be summarized here. Most of these studies were based on self-report data. For example, Klemke's (1982a) study of high school students revealed that lower-class youth reported more recent shoplifting (a moderate inverse relationship, gamma = $-.26$). A similar study of high school youth in a southern community also reported a moderate inverse relationship ($r = -.18$) between social class and self-reported shoplifting (Bales, 1982). Other studies found only a weak inverse relationship. Finally, some studies revealed high levels of shoplifting in various deviant (drug addict) segments of the underclass. Overall, these findings lend slight to modest support for Merton's structural prediction that there should be more deviance among lower-class individuals.

Switching to the individual (micro) level, one of my own respondents from a blue-collar family illustrates the economic deprivation motivation and Merton's classic innovation response. She described her desires for fashionable clothes that would help enhance her chances of being accepted by the popular kids in her junior and senior high school. Unfortunately, these items were often far beyond the limits of the family budget. Because she was unable to purchase them, shoplifting became a way of obtaining the designer jeans and other stylish items that she craved. She said, "I'd go on sprees. Once I'd taken something I'd want to go back and take something else. Because it was like, look what I have! And I never thought I could have that cause I didn't have the money. That was the point, I didn't have the money and I couldn't buy it."

Many critics have questioned Merton's view that delinquents are most likely to be experiencing frustration in attaining their high level of *future* success (e.g., Liska, 1971; Kornhauser, 1978; Elliott et al., 1985). A noteworthy challenge and qualification emerged from the Schwendingers' (1985) extensive field research on adolescent subcultures. They found that most of the highly delinquent junior-high-school subjects exhibited very little concern about future occupations. Instead, the Schwendingers felt that marginal youth were resourcefully creating illegal markets (through shoplifting, drug sales, etc.) to enhance their *immediate* consumption standards in the context of a capitalistic economy.

On the micro level, how important are economic factors in motivating individual shoplifting behavior? There has been considerable debate on this issue. Analysts who stress that economic factors are crucial point to the evidence that most shoplifters, like other frugal customers, are seeking to enhance their financial situation. Besides Merton, theorists reviving the rational choice theoretical explanation of criminal behavior have also fostered this view (Cornish and Clarke, 1986). These theorists apply micro-economic models to analyze criminal decision making. The individual who contemplates shoplifting will attempt to assess (1) the rewards (economic, social, and psychological), and (2) the risks (getting caught) and costs (punishments) that might be incurred. (This perspective will be developed more extensively later in the chapter.) Individuals may shoplift because of economic need (being in a poor financial condition), economic greed (feeling relative deprivation), or just because it is perceived to be an easy means of obtaining desirable items.[5]

Strong economic motivations have been uncovered in many field studies of shoplifters (Yates, 1986). Anne Campbell (1981), for example, interviewed delinquent girls in England. Her respondents repeatedly articulated how important economic motivations were for their high involvement in shoplifting. Instead of pathological personalities, she found that "consumer fetishism" seemed to be driving many of these young, working class females into shoplifting. At the macro level, and sounding like Merton, she points to how the fashion industry, stores, and media bombard these poor girls into desiring the ever-changing "ideal" styles of dress, cosmetics, jewelry, and so on that promise to enhance their personal identity and romantic potential. Campbell found that when these highly desired products are not within reach of one's meager budget, individuals may resort to shoplifting to acquire them.

A team of researchers (Carpenter et al., 1988) conducted an intensive interview study of youth in "Yule City" (a medium-sized city in New York State). These investigators were particularly interested in the connections between drug involvement and crime. They obtained a sample of 100 youth (demographically similar to the state's population) including those with and without drug experiences. Serious efforts were made to obtain insight into the youths' view of their daily experience. The findings are presented in *Kids, Drugs, and Crime*. The chapter titled "Theft and the Consumerist Mentality" is most relevant, as shoplifting was one of the more popular types of theft. The authors present many interview excerpts to support their claim that:

The main impetus the adolescents cited for their thefts (and the thefts of others) was the desire to acquire what they wanted or needed. Money is the main means of exchange by which they acquire goods and services, and lack of money for items they wanted or needed was cited by the majority of youths as the reason behind their thefts. (Carpenter et al., 1988: 62)

A similar study by Terry Williams and William Kornblum (1985), *Growing Up Poor*, was conducted in four cities. They also documented the pervasive economic motives underlying the extensive involvement of economically deprived youth in the underground economy (crime, shoplifting, drugs, etc.).

In another study of high school youth (Klemke, 1982a), respondents were asked to identify their most important reason for shoplifting. The respondents could either select from a set of motivations provided on the questionnaire or write in a response. Two main clusters of motivations were selected by the youth who had shoplifted. The first cluster encompassed primarily *economic* motivations. It was selected by 45.1 percent of the shoplifters: 24.1 percent "needed something and couldn't afford to pay for it," 20.7 percent "wanted the item and didn't want to pay for it," and 0.3 percent cited "to get items to sell". The second cluster was called *sporting* motivations. It was frequently chosen, with 42.4 percent of the shoplifters identifying motivations of this type: 29.2 percent "to see if they could get away with it," and 13.2 percent "for fun and excitement."[6] Only a few of the shoplifters selected the *peer pressure* motivation item: 5.9 percent cited "because friends were doing it." However, peer pressure is undoubtedly also important in stimulating and supporting the economic and sporting motivations. Otherwise, only 3.2 percent of the shoplifters selected the *illicit market* motivation ("taking items they could not buy, such as cigarettes and beer") and 3.5 percent wrote in a special response. In conclusion, *economic and non-economic reasons were almost equally selected as important motivations by these adolescent shoplifters.*

All the subjects in these studies were juveniles, and many came from lower-class families. Thus, there may be more "objective" economic deprivation than might be found in more affluent or adult subjects.

However, sociologists have been sensitive to the possibility that most people in our acquisitive-capitalistic society feel unsatisfied with their accumulation of material possessions.[7] Echoing Merton, Cameron made this explicit in her analysis of affluent adult female shoplifters. She claimed that:

The middle-class itself cannot always achieve middle-class goals by legitimate means. The frustration is not so profound as in the lower-class, however, and the individual thefts of middle-class people are sometimes of small magnitude, but middle-class people do try theft as a means to bridge the gap between earnings and "needs" and many of them are at least temporarily successful. (Cameron, 1964: 173)

This is also reminiscent of Donald Cressey's (1971) finding that *non-shareable financial problems* preceded the acts of embezzlement committed by his white collar convicted male respondents.

Finally, even though the evidence is very sparse, economic motivations appear to be stronger for adults and semi-professional shoplifters. Both of these types are presumed to be making more calculated economic decisions than juveniles or non-professional shoplifters (Ray and Briar, 1988). This is very evident in the studies of drug addicts (presented in Chapter 3) that revealed reliance on shoplifting as a major way of financing their legitimate and illegitimate life-styles. One of the few existing descriptive accounts of a former semi-professional shoplifter (Klokis, 1985) also emphasizes the importance of the financial payoff. He describes the calculating tactics of his booster team, which stole up to $8,000 in merchandise a day. Moore's semi-professional shoplifters (shoplifting more frequently and more expensive items) may view shoplifting as their "full-time" or more likely their "part-time" job (Miller, 1978). Kenneth Tunnell (1992) conducted an interview study of active adult property offenders (many had been active shoplifters at some time in their criminal career). He discovered that financial motivations were nearly universally claimed to be the primary reason for their criminal acts. Finally, in a study of adult shoplifters, Yates (1986) found that two-thirds were primarily motivated by financial incentives.

On the other hand, many analysts of shoplifting consider non-economic factors to be more significant than economic factors. These scholars point to the irrational non-utilitarian behavior exhibited by some (or most, depending on the writer) shoplifters. As discussed earlier in this chapter, psychologists and psychiatrists are especially likely to formulate non-economic explanations for shoplifting behavior. Security personnel frequently downplay the importance of economic motivations because many apprehended shoplifters (1) steal inexpensive items and (2) carry financial resources (cash, checks, or credit cards) that could have been used to pay for the stolen merchandise (Edwards, 1970; Baumer and Rosenbaum, 1984).

Sociologists have also uncovered evidence that more than economic issues underlie criminal behavior. This is very evident in Erving Goffman's (1967) classic essay, "Where the Action Is," in which he presents an insightful analysis of legitimate and illegitimate risk-taking behavior.[8] Crime, for example, can be a way of demonstrating one's courage, gameness, integrity, and ability to perform under pressure that may not be possible by legitimate behavior. Individuals may therefore "seek out" involvements like shoplifting because of their high "action" potential.[9]

Ethnographic, questionnaire, and interview studies on how individuals account for their shoplifting behavior have revealed a complex range of motivations. As noted previously, Klemke (1982a) discovered that about half the high school shoplifters selected non-economic (sporting and peer pressure) motivations as the main reason for their shoplifting. Almost every analyst of shoplifting, particularly those studying juveniles, has found significant evidence of expressive, non-utilitarian motives.

The single most important challenge to economic-based explanations has been developed by Jack Katz. In *Seductions of Crime*, Katz (1988) specifically critiques the Mertonian explanations. He claims that the theories that stress structural and background factors do not adequately explain why and how a particular crime is committed. To pursue this issue he feels that researchers must adopt a phenomenological perspective and study the respondent's "definition of the situation" before and during the commission of a crime. Therefore, he analyzes accounts of shoplifting obtained from his primarily female, upper middle class criminology students at the University of California, Los Angeles. He claims that, at least for these students, material needs are often clearly insufficient to account for involvement in theft and shoplifting. To support his alternative viewpoint, he points to the "seductive power of objects," "cheap thrills," and the "profoundly moving experience" that his subjects referred to when describing why they had shoplifted (Katz, 1988). More specifically, he summarizes five different types of thrills or challenges articulated by his subjects: (1) providing a test of what and who you are; (2) a kind of game; (3) a religious (a secret defilement or black sacrament) experience; (4) a sexual experience; and (5) a vehicle for discovering charisma (a personal esthetic triumph). In addition, Richard Mitchell (1984) has emphasized how deviance is often a meaningful experience whereby alienated individuals can express their creativity and individuality. Shoplifting can be a very engaging way of enhancing one's experiences and discovering new and different ways of being.[10] It may be repeated to regain the thrill and euphoria experienced in prior escapades.

It is very difficult to summarize the diverse evidence on the value of anomie-strain theory and economic motivations for understanding shoplifting. As Margaret Farnsworth and Michael Leiber (1989) and Mitchell (1984) have pointed out, much of the controversy is rooted in different interpretations and conceptualizations of Merton's original ideas. Farnsworth and Lieber's research on Seattle youth, utilizing a more precise operationalization of Merton's ideas, led them to conclude that strain was a good predictor of delinquency. Likewise, the preceding discussion suggests that strain at a structural level and economic motivations at a personal level can be useful in understanding shoplifting. Obviously, the two levels are interactive and often reinforce one another. It is important to keep in mind, however, that the evidence for non-economic motivations is almost as strong. Any particular act of shoplifting probably has *both* economic and non-economic motivations. The importance of each of these types of motivations will vary dramatically from case to case.

SOCIAL CONTROL THEORIES—FAMILY AND SCHOOL FOCUSED—AND SHOPLIFTING

The second major perspective has generally been referred to as social control theories. Almost a century ago, Durkheim (1951) discovered that individuals who were poorly integrated into the society or who had their social bonds to society broken (e.g., because of a divorce or loss of employment) were more likely to commit suicide. Since then sociologists have continued to study how individuals are woven into a social fabric of the society.

The most important contemporary advocate of this theoretical tradition has been Travis Hirschi (1969). His research supported the theory that individuals with weak social bonds (attachments, beliefs, involvements, and commitments to the social order) would be more delinquent. In a recent theoretical effort, Gottfredson and Hirschi (1990) stress the importance of low "self-control" as a general explanatory variable. Unfortunately, only limited empirical shoplifting research is available to evaluate the merits of parts of these versions of social control theory.

Other social control theorists have hypothesized that individuals who experience major conflicts, disruptions, and/or failures in their social relationships would be more likely to commit crime-deviance. These sociologists have examined the main social worlds that an individual occupies for conditions that might weaken or strengthen commitment to the legitimate social order. Ivan Nye (1958) and Hirschi (1969), for example, carefully studied the social world of the family and how family relationships might be related to delinquency involvements. Likewise, Hirschi (1969), Walter Schafer and Kenneth Polk (1967), and Michael

Wiatrowski et al. (1981) have identified the social world of the school as being a crucial arena for how youth's lives unfold.[11] At this time, specific research on how an individual's relationships within the family and school might be connected to shoplifting will be reviewed. Some of the research is explicitly based on social control theory; some is only marginally within this tradition.

Sociologists and psychologists have long considered the family to be an important potential source of deviant behavior. Psychologists attempting to explain deviance have typically placed more weight on the family than have sociologists. Their theories have emphasized different dimensions than those cited by social control theorists. For example, they have particularly stressed *early experiences* in the family as being crucial in the development of mental health. Undesirable family experiences and influences are likely to result in vulnerable individuals who resort to deviant behavior patterns. John Bowlby (1947), for example, conducted a study of children who had been referred to the London Child Guidance Clinic. He compared 44 children who had serious theft problems with children referred to the clinic for other types of problems. The most significant difference between the two groups was that the thieves had experienced a higher incidence of prolonged separations from their mothers during the first five years of their lives. Several other examples of this line of thinking have been presented in the psychological section of this chapter.

G. R. Patterson, a behavioral psychologist (1980), developed a different type of family-centered theory. His essay "Children Who Steal" was based on small samples of children who had been manifesting chronic problems and their families. He was particularly interested in how these parents and children interacted with each other. His research revealed that the parents of chronic thieves were not strongly attached to their children (control theory) and were less likely to punish (social learning theory) their children for earlier misbehavior. Having "gotten away" with lying and being out of control, the children progressed to stealing. They continued stealing the things they wanted because they had been successful in avoiding negative consequences for prior thefts.

The sociological social control theorists have spent a great deal of effort to uncover how family factors are related to juvenile delinquency. For example, F. Ivan Nye's (1958) early research found that delinquency was more strongly related to the *quality* of family relationships than to the *structural* features of the family. More recently, Karen Wilkinson (1980) explored the importance of being in a structurally broken home (natural father not in the home). This study is one of the few family-centered analyses that looks at shoplifting. Her research of a large high school sample showed that girls, but not boys, from broken homes were somewhat more likely to shoplift. More specifically, shoplifting was more frequent for girls from broken homes that were Mexican-American as opposed to Anglo-American, Catholic as opposed to Protestant, and rural as opposed to urban. She concluded that where there was less "divorce tolerance" there would be more trauma generated by a divorce. This seemed to explain why there was more shoplifting among girls, Mexican-Americans, Catholics, and rural residents when a family did break up.

W. A. Belson's (1975) in-depth study of stealing among a large sample of boys in London evaluated the importance of family variables. He found that boys who disliked being at home were more likely to be involved in different kinds of thefts. Klemke (1982a) looked more specifically at how the quality of family relationships affected shoplifting activity for a large sample of high school youth. Youth who had unfavorable relationships with their parents were somewhat more likely to shoplift. "Getting along with" one's father was more important for males, while "getting along with" the mother was more important for females. All these quantitative studies report a moderate relationship between certain family variables and shoplifting activity. Finally, a study of middle-class youth (Richards et al., 1979) found that several indicators of family conflict were moderately related to shoplifting. The relationship was strongest for elementary school students and became successively weaker for junior high and high school students. The researchers did not, however, find a significant relationship between being from a broken home and shoplifting. Similarly, Bales's (1982) research on high school students did not find a relationship between parental marital status and shoplifting.

Qualitative evidence on links between family factors and shoplifting fosters a greater understanding of the social dynamics that are involved. In Shaw's case studies (of Stanley in *The Jack-Roller* and of Sidney in *The Natural History of a Delinquent Career*), the respondents provide numerous examples of maltreatment at the hands of their parents or a stepparent. He suggests that these poor relationships led to "hanging out" with older delinquent youth, running away, shoplifting (Sidney had eight shoplifting arrests and Stanley had three), and other types of delinquency. In these cases, weak social bonds in the family created conditions conducive to exploring and developing delinquency patterns.

This was also evident in one of my own respondents, a female from an upper middle class family. She placed considerable weight on being ignored by her father, a busy high school principal, and being used as a housekeeper by her mother to explain why she turned to shoplifting during her high school years. Another respondent's father was an alcoholic; this injected a great deal of strife and resentment into the family unit during the time that she was involved in shoplifting. A third respondent had good family relationships until early adolescence, then "all hell broke loose." She particularly identified changes in her behavior (e.g., drug use, skipping school, getting into fights, and shoplifting) when she joined a rowdy peer group in her new junior high school. In contrast to the other examples, she felt it was mainly *her* fault that the social bonds in her family were deteriorating. These examples highlight the complex interactions whereby youth can be both a social product of and an active influence on the family life situation.

Unfortunately, all the literature on family factors and shoplifting just cited has concentrated on children and youth. This is obviously the phase of the life-cycle at which family influences might be most apparent. Family influences do not stop after adolescence, however. Security personnel, journalists, and psychologists claim that marital/sexual problems seem to trigger shoplifting by *adults*, and particularly by *female* adults. Yates (1986) did find a high rate of family conflict in her specialized sample of convicted shoplifters (who had been referred to a probation department for psychological assessments). Much better research on more representative samples is urgently needed to clarify and confirm these relationships.

The school, being a central involvement for youth, has also been emphasized by social control theorists (Hirschi, 1969). However, most studies fail to look specifically at how school variables are related to shoplifting. Ironically, the few studies that do explore this relationship have not been conducted by social control theorists. In one of these, a study of middle-class youth (Richards et al., 1979), several school indicators were moderately related to shoplifting. Specifically, youth who had poor academic performances, unfavorable attitudes toward school, and more anger toward school officials were significantly more likely to shoplift. The only other study targeting the relationship between school experiences and shoplifting is presented by Klemke (1982a). He found that a student's grade performance and attitudes toward school were significantly and inversely related to recent shoplifting. Belson's (1975) study of boys in London also reported a strong relationship between truancy and theft involvements.

Ironically, the very scanty interview material on this issue suggests that schools may not be as important as the correlations imply. In Shaw's case studies, for example, schools are mentioned only in a peripheral way. It appears that his subjects were too committed to life on the streets and their delinquent peers to give much serious attention to school. Several of my own respondents also downplayed the importance of school in their lives. They saw their problems at school as being just another indicator of their conflict with the system rather than a cause of their problems. Few youth articulate the classic "status frustration" pattern theorized by Albert Cohen (1955). Instead, they perceive that they are failing because *they* did not pay attention, study, or attend; not because schools were discriminating against them.[12] It was their own fault, not the school's; they had more exciting things to do! Here again it becomes a challenge to untangle and understand the relationships between school and shoplifting. Unlike school vandalism, there is no inherent reason why a youth's disenchantment with school would be specifically manifested in shoplifting behavior. Longitudinal research may be necessary to ascertain the causal sequencing between school variables and shoplifting.

In conclusion, there is rather consistent quantitative and qualitative support for the proposition that weak social bonds in the family are moderately related to shoplifting. The research on school bonds and shoplifting is less consistent. While the quantitative research shows strong inverse relationships between school variables and shoplifting, the limited qualitative evidence downplays the impact of school on shoplifting. One hopes that better quality and *more* qualitative research pursuing connections between schools and shoplifting will clarify this issue. In the meantime, it seems safe to conclude that shoplifting, like many other types of delinquency, is more frequently committed by youth who are less strongly bound to the social order (family and school). How and if these relationships apply to adults and shoplifting is still unexplored and will require major new research efforts.

SOCIALIZATION-REINFORCEMENT THEORIES AND SHOPLIFTING

Socialization theories add a new dimension to the study of deviance. While social control theories focus on the *quality of one's relationships*, socialization theorists are more concerned with the *content of what one learns* from one's significant others. One of the most influential sociological theories—and the most important criminal socialization theory—is Edwin Sutherland's differential association theory (Sutherland and Cressey, 1970). Like the Chicago School sociologists, Sutherland was very interested in how individual and social influences interacted; therefore, his theory is also considered to be an "interactionist theory." He stressed that criminal behavior is often a product of cultural transmission. One's associates tend to shape one's views on what is acceptable behavior. Crime is sometimes a part of the cultural tradition of a community, or of a subculture within the community. Therefore, individuals may be socialized by deviant significant others about specific crime techniques and attitudes necessary to commit criminal acts. More specifically, Sutherland stated that the earlier, more frequently, and longer one is exposed to criminal patterns endorsed by individuals whom one really cares about, the greater the likelihood that one will also manifest these criminal patterns. Shoplifters who are operating within the context of a group or subculture fit this pattern and are prime examples of the "systematic" deviant type identified by Lemert (see Chapter 4).

Other theorists have modified or developed variations of Sutherland's theory. Sociologists Robert Burgess and Ronald Akers (1966) and Akers (1985) have revised Sutherland's original formulation to incorporate social learning or reinforcement principles. They weave positive reinforcement and negative reinforcement variables into Sutherland's interactionist theory. Akers reports on his empirical research on adolescent drug use that supports the theoretical perspective. He has also written on how this perspective is applicable to all types of deviance. Patterson (1980), a psychologist, provides another good example of the behavioral (operant conditioning and social learning) perspective.

Many quantitative research projects have been devoted to the socialization perspective. Using many of the variables identified by Sutherland, Belson examined patterns of juvenile theft (including shoplifting) for a large sample of British boys. He concluded that stealing increased with the proportion of one's associates who were thieves; the amount of stealing done by these associates; the length of time one associated with thieves; and whether they had associated with thieves at an early age (Belson, 1975).

Research by Klemke (1982a) explored whether high school respondents had knowledge of shoplifting by various significant others (parents, siblings, and close friends). Approximately 3 percent of the youth were aware of parental shoplifting, 28 percent knew of sibling shoplifting, and 57 percent knew of shoplifting by close friends. The relationships between knowledge of shoplifting by significant others and recent shoplifting were all very strong (e.g., the gammas ranged from .47 when a brother was known to have shoplifted to .82 when one's close friends were known to have shoplifted). Therefore, when shoplifting is present in one's immediate social networks, there is a high likelihood that deviant socialization will occur. Because the data are cross-sectional it is impossible to unequivocally establish the causal pattern, but it is clear that a great deal of potential socialization and reinforcement of shoplifting exists when one's significant others are shoplifting.

Additional data generally reinforce confidence in the deviant socialization thesis. For example, Bales (1982) conducted a modest study of shoplifting in a random sample of youth in a small southern community. He attempted to assess the importance of three theoretical perspectives in understanding the decision to shoplift: differential association, economic decision making, and the deterrence perspective. His data showed that the differential association variables were most strongly related to shoplifting. Kraut's (1976) study of college students concluded that those who knew that their friends shoplifted or approved of shoplifting were much more likely to shoplift. Of all the independent variables considered, the peer support variables produced the largest correlations with shoplifting behavior.[13] Similarly, the Richards et al. (1979) study of suburban youth confirmed that knowing peers who shoplifted was the strongest predictor of shoplifting.

Consistent with Sutherland's ideas, a great deal of delinquency actually occurs in the company of other youth (Erickson, 1973). The "group" often appears to be instrumental in initiating, facilitating, and rewarding many criminal acts. Shoplifting, particularly that committed by young people and adult "professionals" (recall the examples of shoplifting teams and troupes in Chapter 2), has repeatedly been found to take place with accomplices. Cameron (1964) noted, without providing specific statistics, that apprehended adult shoplifters were almost uniformly alone, while apprehended juveniles were usually with others of the same sex and age. A high rate of young shoplifters being apprehended with an accomplice has been noted frequently in other studies of store records. Robin's study of department stores (1963) found that 75.3 percent of the juveniles and 23.3 percent of the adults apprehended for shoplifting were with at least one other person. Brady and Mitchell's Melbourne department store data (1971) showed very similar patterns. They found that 81.3 percent of those apprehended under age 20 were with accomplices (4.1% with a family member and 77.2% with friends), but only 24 percent of those over age 20 were with an accomplice (9.4% with a family member and 14.5% with friends).

Because apprehension data may incorporate what has been called a group-hazard bias (i.e., delinquent acts with multiple offenders may be more likely to be detected), researchers have turned to self-report studies (Erickson, 1973). This type of research has, in fact, generally found smaller numbers of young shoplifters being accompanied by others than store apprehension research indicates (there are no systematic self-report data on this issue for adults). Gold (1970), for example, noted that shoplifting in Flint, Michigan, was often committed by youth with another youth (specific statistics were not presented). More specifically, Klemke (1982a) found that 60.7 percent of high school students who have shoplifted, reported having done at least some shoplifting with a companion. Maynard Erickson and Gary Jensen's (1977) self-report study of high school students in six different types of schools and communities presents the lowest percentage of "group" involvement in shoplifting. Even so, Erickson and Jensen still found that 50 percent of the 2,869 reported incidents of shoplifting were done with another person. Females were somewhat more likely to report shoplifting with companions (60%) than were males (44%). Finally, in a study of British youth between age 11 and 14, J. Shapland (1978) found "group" involvement in shoplifting to be similar to the pattern found in store apprehension studies. She reports that companions were involved in 63 percent of the shoplifting incidents from small shops and in 75.4 percent of the incidents from large stores.

Therefore, there is strong evidence that others, particularly peers, are often involved in incidents of *juvenile* shoplifting. Regardless of the research approach, between 50 percent and 81.3 percent of the youth who have shoplifted report doing it with accomplices.

Qualitative research adds further verification and insight into the dynamics of the social processes identified by the socialization-reinforcement theorists. This is evident in many interview accounts of young shoplifters describing how they began and why they continue to shoplift. Shaw's life histories contained numerous examples of shoplifting socialization-reinforcement experiences provided by significant others. Recall the accounts of Sidney and Stanley in Chapter 2 of slightly older peers, siblings, and even stepparents instructing, prompting, and encouraging their shoplifting behavior. The rich detail found in interview material is particularly valuable in revealing the specific and varied roles that significant others may play in stimulating, facilitating, and rewarding shoplifting behavior. Illustrative examples of how these social processes are manifested might be helpful.

One of my own interview respondents gave a detailed account (presented in Chapter 2) of how her high school "parking lot group" would periodically ditch school and engage in shoplifting contests. They would return at the end of the school day to see who had come up with the best accumulation of loot in one afternoon, and thereby win the contest. Many youth have another person(s) with them for personal support (one of my young respondents reported that having colleagues with him bolstered his courage). Sophisticated shoplifters realize that having accomplices who can distract a clerk's attention or serve as a lookout can enhance their chance of success. Several accounts by "professional" adult shoplifters presented in Chapter 2 document this pattern. Belson's research showed that youth claimed thieving (like doing drugs and vandalism) was "more fun" when it was a shared group experience. In real-life variations of Solomon Asch's famous group-pressure experiments (1951), I have had respondents report that they participated in a shoplifting incident only because they were coerced by peers. Likewise, I have heard of stories (this was a long time ago) of teenage "Jarman Sweater Clubs" in which membership initiation required the theft of a sweater. More recently, Jeff Farrell (1990) reports that one of the strong norms of New York City "graffiti artists" is to shoplift the cans of spray paint used in the production of their artwork.

The important role that others may play in shoplifting is also manifested in cases in which the line between shoplifting and employee theft becomes blurred. Typically, a friend or relative who works in a store will agree ahead of time to "look the other way" or "not ring up" all the items that the "shopper" takes out of the store. There will often be a sharing of the merchandise or promise of other payoffs to the "inside" person.[14] Another variation occurs when former employees, being knowledgeable about a store's security system, personnel, and procedures, exploit this information in future shoplifting episodes. One of my own respondents described how members of his active high school shoplifting group deliberately sought part-time and summer jobs in particular stores so that they could obtain information and have an inside person to minimize their risks. He said, "Once a person knows how the security is set up, you can then steal anything you want." He gave specific examples of valuable information derived from his insider friends about the vulnerability of particular stores. They learned that security personnel in one store started working at 11:00 A.M., giving them two hours of "safe time" to shoplift. From another insider they learned that only store security personnel could make an apprehension— and only when they had personally witnessed the shoplifting act. This greatly minimized the risk, especially when one knew the identity of the security personnel! Likewise, knowing the store's policy on returning merchandise (a frequent mode of converting shoplifted items into cash), the presence and use of security technology, location of hidden observation spots, and so forth is tremendously valuable. Because many stores are part of a larger chain, knowledge about one store can make shoplifting at other branch locations less risky. Reports from a number of my respondents suggest that collusion and sharing of inside information by present and former employees is more prevalent than has previously been acknowledged.

Finally, shoplifting has at times been the central reason for forming a group (recall Manny being recruited and trained by the female fur booster in Chapter 2). Police periodically uncover shoplifting organizations (Baumer and Rosenbaum, 1984). Recently a ring of young shoplifters, recruited and instructed by a "modern-day Fagin," was arrested. At least 42 children, age 11 to 14 and from four states, were implicated in this group. They carried a four-page training manual of detailed instructions on how to steal, what items to take, what to do if they got caught, and a listing of targeted malls (*Juvenile Justice Digest*, 1987). Another shoplifting ring led by a Spokane, Washington, couple was uncovered by police (*The Oregonian*, 1991). Nineteen individuals were linked to this group, which had been stealing items on order for five years.

There may also be generalized support for shoplifting in neighborhoods in which there is a "theft subculture." Mayhew's (1968) depiction of nineteenth-century London slums portrayed an extensive underworld where pickpockets, shoplifters, and other types of thieves abounded.

Similar scenarios are found in Asbury's description of the underworld of New York City in the 1800s (1927) and the Chicago slums studied by Shaw and McKay (see Chapter 2). Contemporary ethnographic studies of slum communities also find an abundance of illegitimate economic opportunities pervading the cultural landscape. Bernard Rosenberg and Harry Silverstein (1969) claim that nearly every youngster in the slum areas that they studied in New York, Washington, and Chicago has developed some kind of "larceny sense." Homes, apartments, cars, shops in the neighborhood, and downtown department stores were the primary targets. These authors found petty shoplifting to be nearly universal among slum youth. Jagna Sharff (1981) conducted a field study of a Hispanic slum neighborhood. She mapped out how residents resourcefully blended legitimate work, welfare, and illegitimate work (drug traffic, illegal lottery, burglary, shoplifting, fencing, etc.) in order to keep themselves on the thin and precarious financial tightrope that they had to traverse each day.

Spergle's study of Chicago communities, *Racketville, Slumtown, and Haulburg* (1964), is also instructive. In these communities a theft subculture provided mobility options to juvenile burglars, shoplifters, and other such youth to move into the ranks of adult semi-professional and professional thieves. The social organization of these communities also included fences to facilitate the transfer of "hot" goods into cash. While many fences do not want to develop a heavy reliance on "penny-ante thieves" (such as most shoplifters), they do buy from them when the items are of good quality and they can get a good deal (Steffensmeier, 1986; Klockars, 1974). Marilyn Walsh's study of 90 fences found that only 12 percent regularly relied on boosters (1978). More frequently, shoplifters serve as their own fences. Especially in communities with a theft subculture, shoplifters can easily sell their goods to friends, neighbors, patrons of a bar, and so forth, or trade them for drugs or other desired commodities or services (Anderson, 1976). This process was frequently observed by a team of field researchers (Johnson et al., 1985) as described in Booster Box 7. Besides documenting the pervasive amount and subcultural support of shoplifting in this poor community, the excerpt reemphasizes the importance of economic motivations mentioned earlier in this chapter. In fact, the authors came to view shoplifting as an unorthodox form of "involuntary welfare payment" from the stores to the poor residents of the community.

Booster Box 7
STREET-LEVEL FENCING

Stolen goods are a major component of the ghetto economy. Subjects who engaged in shoplifting or other forms of theft seldom sold the goods they stole to professional fences. Most often, they sold the goods to other neighborhood residents directly. This process was graphically illustrated time after time at the research storefront. The research staff were not generally offered drugs for purchase, but they were frequently asked to buy stolen merchandise. Subjects would come to the storefront with stacks of shirts, boxes of film, a wristwatch, other jewelry, and try to sell them to staff. More often, the staff were solicited by strangers who would wander into the storefront with an armful of new designer jeans, an automobile battery, a radio, an assortment of leather belts, and so forth and offer them for sale. Subjects awaiting interviews frequently examined the merchandise and made purchases, at substantial discounts, of items they might not otherwise have been able to afford. Some research subjects, sensitive to our presence, would invite the seller outside and make the purchase in the street. When they came back inside, they would proudly show off their new possessions to other subjects and field staff alike.

After leaving the storefront, the sellers would continue down the street, entering the beauty parlor, a hamburger joint, a social club, or soliciting passersby.

Source: Bruce D. Johnson et al. 1985. *Taking Care of Business: The Economics of Crime by Heroin Abusers*. Lexington, Mass.: Lexington Books: 118–19)

Many other studies of slum communities and street drug addicts, as discussed in Chapter 3, reveal high levels of shoplifting activity (e.g., Inciardi, 1980; Prus and Irini, 1980; Miller, 1986; Kowalski and Faupel, 1990). Shoplifting is often a major component of the larger street culture of drugs, prostitution, and crime. Clearly, shoplifting may become an important economic survival tactic within this subculture and may pave the way for entrance into and maintenance of drug involvements.[15]

There are also examples of pro-shoplifting attitudes and norms within subcultures of the more affluent sectors of the society. Examples were given in Chapter 2 of shoplifting by middle-class youth (Weiner, 1970) and of Abbie Hoffman promoting an attack on the capitalist society by ripping off stores (Hoffman, 1989). Research on adolescent subcultures (Schwendinger and Schwendinger, 1985) uncovered illegal markets in all social class levels of American society. More of this type of research is needed to ascertain the subcultural support for shoplifting in the more affluent social classes. Such research might alter the existing findings that suggest that there is more support for shoplifting in the underclass sector of society.

While Sutherland stressed the importance of being socialized by one's significant others, it is also possible to be influenced by impersonal media sources. For example, David Phillips (1974) and Kenneth Bollen and Phillips (1982) have found that the highly publicized reporting of a famous person's suicide may stimulate a slight increase in the national suicide rate. Many people believe that the music world (from Elvis and the Beatles to Madonna, etc.) has a great influence on contemporary youth culture. While one should be very cautious about imputing too much influence to this source, it is interesting to see shoplifting being glamorized and legitimated in a song by the popular rock group Jane's Addiction (see Booster Box 8).

Booster Box 8
JANE'S ADDICTION

In the song *Been Caught Stealing* by Jane's Addiction, a male youth describes being caught for shoplifting when he was five years old. However, this does not deter him from becoming a repetitive shoplifter who simply takes items that he does not want to pay for. His girlfriend also takes items from stores, and her technique of hiding things under her skirt is detailed. It is also pointed out that they do this together. Finally, it is reiterated throughout how enjoyable the acts are, and as it repeats at the end of each stanza, "If I get by, it's mine, all mine!"

All these studies indicate that various individuals and social processes within one's primary groups and neighborhoods may stimulate, support, and reward shoplifting activity. Collectively, they provide strong evidence that Sutherland's differential association theory (and Burgess and Akers's reinforcement version) significantly enhances our understanding of shoplifting behavior.

On the other hand, there are obvious limitations to the socialization-reinforcement perspective. First, it does not explain Lemert's "individual" shoplifters (e.g., psychologically/psychiatrically disordered shoplifters). This is not too significant a problem, as only a small number of shoplifters fit this type. Second, most shoplifting techniques are not very complicated. Therefore, unlike safecracking and complex confidence games, extensive socialization is not a prerequisite. Individuals can begin, and even continue, shoplifting without instigation by others. Because there has been no systematic study of how individuals begin to shoplift, a question was included in my own survey of a convenience sample of college students. They were asked whether they had "discovered how to shoplift by themselves" or "heard or learned how to do it from someone." It is interesting that 47 percent claimed to have discovered the practice on their own, while 53 percent recalled picking up the idea from others. The significant number who have independently discovered shoplifting clashes with the classic deviant socialization pattern. It should be kept in mind that the data come from a small and non-random sample of college students. Likewise, the respondents' recall ability was being stretched, because the first shoplifting act often occurs during childhood.[16] Still, the finding provides an initial point of comparison and suggests that much more research should focus on the initial act of shoplifting.

Finally, Cameron (1964) suggests that the differential association perspective is of limited value in explaining the behavior of middle-class female shoplifters. Because these shoplifters did not have criminal records or criminal subcultural associations, she felt that differential association was not relevant. This may be true for their present situation and, therefore, could pose a challenge to Sutherland's theory. The reinforcement theoretical perspective may be more helpful in explaining these types of shoplifters. Such "independent" shoplifters may continue because they receive a variety of financial, social, and psychological rewards from their deviance (Katz, 1988). Shoplifting can even continue in the absence of general social factors (anomie, lack of social controls, etc.) that typically push individuals toward deviant modes of adaptations.[17] The evidence accumulated in this chapter suggests that few shoplifters would fit this pattern.

It is also likely that many active middle-class female shoplifters have had peer-supported shoplifting involvements during their youth. Thus, even though they are currently freelancing, previous differential association shoplifting influences may make their present behavior more understandable. More detailed research is needed to establish the influences that operate at different phases of the life-cycle and at different stages of a shoplifting career.

NEUTRALIZATION THEORY AND SHOPLIFTING

The next sociological theoretical perspective to be covered is the neutralization theory of Gresham Sykes and David Matza (1957). Theirs is really an elaboration and development of a statement from Sutherland's theory that individuals can learn criminal techniques and the "motives, drives, rationalizations, and attitudes favorable to the violation of the law" (Sutherland and Cressey, 1970: 76). Sykes and Matza's analysis also overlaps with social control theory because it emphasizes how individuals, at least temporarily, evade the normative order of the society.

According to Sykes and Matza, many delinquents (1) maintain some commitment to the dominant social order, and therefore (2) must invoke techniques of neutralizations (denial of responsibility, denial of injury, denial of the victim, condemnation of one's condemners, and appeal to higher loyalties) *before* they can violate the law. Both of these ingredients seem to "fit" many shoplifters, particularly those who fit Lemert's "situational" type.[18] Many shoplifters are "respectable" individuals who commit this deviance only in certain situations.

At a simple descriptive level, many shoplifters do articulate classic examples of neutralizations when researchers ask them why they shoplift. When obtained under conditions of anonymity or by a "trusted" researcher, their accounts are usually quite credible. On the other hand, accounts obtained by store security personnel during an emotional apprehension experience are less likely to be honest statements.

Various neutralization techniques, derived from interviews of shoplifters by myself and other researchers, run the full gamut of the types developed by Sykes and Matza. Some poignant examples are presented here. The first is *denial of responsibility*. In these cases, offenders claim that they should not be held accountable for their actions because of extenuating circumstances. A young respondent reported to me that he shoplifted only when he was "under the influence" and had gone into a market to shoplift more beer for an on-going party. Another recounted that she "was too young to realize what I was doing." Many other respondents have reported to me that their only shoplifting occurred when they reluctantly went along or were coerced into it by their shoplifting friends.

Shoplifters often articulate the second type, which Sykes and Matza call *denial of injury* neutralizations. Here offenders minimize the seriousness or wrongness of their shoplifting activity. Norman Weiner (1970), for example, reported middle-class youth frequently speaking of "getting" things (not "stealing" things) when talking about their shoplifting activities. An interesting study of a subculture of ex-mental patients reported that they referred to their shoplifting of food as "doing the groceries" (Herman, 1987). Cameron (1964) noted that most snitches do not think of themselves as thieves or criminals. Another denial of injury neutralization takes the form of minimizing the dollar value of the stolen merchandise: "It was only a cheap bottle of perfume," or "It's such a large store they won't even miss it."

Denial of the victim neutralizations are often used by those who believe that stores are deserving targets. One of my own respondents, a 20-year-old female from an affluent family, had a well-articulated anti-business mindset. She justified her shoplifting, saying:

I felt that the whole system—who owns the stores, who makes the profit—is set up by the same people, the people who have everything. I thought it served them right, they have more than they know what to do with, and they were charging $50.00 for a pair of jeans! Every time I stole something, I'd say, "They rip us off every time we buy something, so I'm just getting even." That's the way I looked at it!

This attitude reflects the anti-establishment shoplifting advocated by Abbie Hoffman. Minorities and ethnic groups may be particularly sensitive to possible discrimination by stores not owned and staffed by fellow group members and may target them for shoplifting (see Booster Box 3 in Chapter 3). Other shoplifters may victimize only one store where they have had a bad experience (e.g., they were overcharged or treated discourteously) and are getting back at the establishment via a form of "economic vandalism." One respondent, for example, returned to shoplift sexy lingerie from a store where she had worked because "I was trying to get back at them for cutting my hours."

Shoplifters express many variations of an *appeal to higher loyalties* neutralization when they claim that other norms and group commitments justify their indiscreet behavior. For example, a youth may resort to shoplifting unaffordable cosmetics and clothes that are deemed "necessary" to enhance his or her attractiveness to the opposite sex. Another person may shoplift food items because he or she is hungry and has no cash. A respondent from Herman's study of ex-mental patients explained that "We only take things from stores when we really need them. Like when we don't have nothing to eat, so we rip off a can of pork and beans. But we don't steal big things like radios or televisions— that would be wrong. We just take food and essential things like that" (Herman, 1987: 248). Similarly, a drug user may feel "compelled" to shoplift to gain the resources for a needed drug purchase. Many shoplifters described by Cameron, and some of my own respondents, stressed how they were taking expensive items to improve their appearance, wardrobe, and so forth and thereby impress others. Several respondents told how they were stealing items to "give away," thus enhancing their reputation as a generous person or simply fulfilling the norm of gift-giving. A newspaper story even described a shoplifter who had taken five Bibles to give away as gifts! There seem to be an endless variety of special reasons, group obligations, and value systems that individuals invoke to justify their shoplifting behavior.

Several quantitative research projects have attempted to evaluate the merits of the neutralization ideas of Sykes and Matza. Two studies (Minor, 1981; Agnew and Peters, 1986) have included questions on shoplifting. Both collected questionnaire data from a sample of college students. Respondents in the Agnew and Peters study were asked if they agreed with items designed to fit various neutralizations (e.g., "I can't afford many things I need very badly," or "Many store owners are dishonest and often cheat customers").[19] In addition, they focused on subjects who disapproved of shoplifting (individuals approving of shop-lifting would not need to invoke neutralizations) in order to target the type of offenders emphasized by Sykes and Matza. As expected, they did find more shoplifting by those who disapproved of shoplifting but agreed with the neutralization items. The relationship became stronger for those who had personally experienced one of the situations specified in the neutralization questionnaire item. After resourceful analyses, the researchers from both projects concluded that neutralization theory does appear to have some explanatory power for shoplifting and other minor types of deviant behavior. They also acknowledged the difficulty of using a questionnaire approach to establish that the individual actually utilized neutralizations *prior* to shoplifting. Interview studies focusing on an individual's thoughts before engaging in a shoplifting incident provide imperfect, but more appropriate, data for evaluating the neutralization theory.

In summary, the review of evidence suggests that the perspective advocated by Sykes and Matza is valuable for studying shoplifting, par-ticularly that which is situational. It is most evident in the examples just presented. While this might be considered "soft" evidence, it is apparent that many individuals believe their shoplifting is a response to atypical situations or pressures, and therefore it does not reflect their real and basically non-criminal character.

RATIONAL CHOICE THEORIES AND SHOPLIFTING

Finally, rational choice theorists have stressed studying criminal be-havior from the perspective of the offender (Piliavin et al., 1986; Tunnell, 1992). These theorists revive the classical tradition in criminology. A recent publication of original papers by psychologists and sociologists, titled *The Reasoning Criminal* (Cornish and Clarke, 1986), provides an excellent introduction to this perspective. All the contributors consider the merits of what they call the rational choice perspective. They feel it is more accurate to regard most offenders as normal persons taking advantage of what they reason are good opportunities for personal gain instead of persons characterized by psychopathology and irrational thinking. Maurice Cusson (1983), for example, emphasizes how indi-viduals perceive that crime will help them attain their personal goals. Like Sykes and Matza (1957) and Katz (1988), rational choice theorists prefer to conduct research that probes what an individual is thinking in the immediate situation surrounding the deviant act.[20] Going beyond Sykes and Matza, they are interested in the individual's *perceptions and calculations of what he or she will gain, and also the risks and costs of embarking on a shoplifting venture*. Rational choice theorists recognize that most criminals have only partial, and often inaccurate, information on the actual rewards and risks associated with a particular crime. Therefore, most of them adopt what is called the limited rationality view of offenders. Two theoretical representations of this approach will be summarized.

Richards, Berk, and Forster (1979) developed a theoretical framework that looks at delinquency from micro-economic principles of decision making and as a meaningful type of leisure activity. They hoped to account for middle-class delinquency (drug use, vandalism, and shoplifting) in a Chicago suburb. The following hypothetical example illustrates their perspective by depicting how a youth might "invest" his or her leisure time in shoplifting a portable radio. Typically, a prospective shoplifter will learn about taking items from more sophisticated friends or will rely on prior personal experiences in risk-taking acts. The youth may also "case" the specific store to anticipate potential problems. If the perceived risks are deemed to be minimal, or if effective counter-strategies can be devised, the decision may be made to take the radio. After the incident, one will weigh the rewards (radio, praise from friends, thrill and excitement of doing it, etc.) against the costs (degree of anxiety while doing it, subsequent guilt feelings, etc.) in deciding whether to do it again (Richards et al., 1979: 29–30).

Regrettably, their research is primarily aimed at establishing the value of the idea of delinquency as a leisure activity, and only minimally at the micro-economic part of their thesis. Nevertheless, the authors conclude that "It is the meshing of needs, resources, rewards, and costs that channel actions, and theories of delinquency cannot afford to limit themselves to the study of predispositions" (Richards et al., 1979: 196).

Other researchers have explored the *cost* component that individuals will be *deterred* from shoplifting when they perceive that there is a high risk of being caught (certainty variable) and/or experience large penalties (severity variable). Kraut's (1976) study of shoplifting supports this contention. He found that shoplifters were less likely than non-shoplifters to perceive that they would be caught and less likely to feel that they would experience serious consequences (e.g., would only be subjected to a lecture by store personnel and not be arrested) if they did happen to be caught. Catherine Cole (1989) found that shoplifters perceived that there was less certainty of their being caught than non-shoplifters, but she did not find any difference for the severity variable. Similar conclusions were also reported by Raymond Patternoster (1989).

In a major critique of this type of research (one-shot survey data), Linda Saltzman et al. (1982) challenged the deterrence interpretation that has been given to this finding. They believe that longitudinal data are necessary to answer the question: Did the perceived lower risk of being caught actually precede the shoplifting (deterrence interpretation), or did the shoplifting precede the perception of low risk (experiential interpretation)? Their longitudinal research, and a replication by W. William Minor and Joseph Harry (1982), found more support for the experiential interpretation and confirms the need to collect data at several points in time to be able to identify the causal order of the variables.

Another example of the rational choice perspective can be found in the imaginative study of shoplifting conducted by John Carroll and Frances Weaver (1986). They generated a simple contingent process model of the decision to shoplift, which is presented in Booster Box 9. To evaluate the meaningfulness of the approach, they developed and implemented the following research procedures. Small samples of "expert" and "novice" shoplifters were recruited. Each agreed to wear a microcassette tape recorder while they "shopped" in stores of their choice.

Booster Box 9
CONTINGENCY PROCESS MODEL OF THE DECISION TO SHOPLIFT

---

1. Assess money in pocket (if high, no crime; if low, go to Step 2);

2. Assess certainty of success (if low, no crime; if high, go to Step 3);

3. Assess amount of gain (if low, go to Step 4; if high, go to Step 5);

4. Assess risk (if high, no crime; if low, go to Step 5);

5. Commit crime (a step that itself would consist of substeps in the planning, selection, and execution of the crime).

Source: John Carroll and Frances Weaver. 1986. "Shoplifters' Perception of Crime Opportunities: A Process-Tracing Study." In Derek B. Cornish and Ronald V. Clarke, eds., *The Reasoning Criminal: Rational Choice Perspectives on Offending.* New York: Springer-Verlag: 23.

Before entering a store, each subject was instructed to form an intention to shoplift (but not to actually do it) and to "think out loud" about this while "shopping" in the store. Each subject was accompanied by a research assistant who would prompt the individual to vocalize what he or she was thinking during long quiet spells. Presumably, the recorded statements captured the individual's thoughts while contemplating whether or not to shoplift. Because the verbal accounts were obtained in such an unstructured manner, it was impossible to make rigorous tests of the propositions and process outlined in Booster Box 9. Instead, content analysis of the verbal protocols led to a suggestive confirmation of the view that the decision to shoplift is fairly rational. The "shoplifters" often vocalized that they were considering the degree of attractiveness, dollar value, and/or need for the items that they were most interested in taking. Most articulated how they were weighing the feasibility and the particular risks that taking the item would entail. Many subjects (particularly the expert shoplifters) also spoke of strategies they would implement to minimize the chance of being apprehended. The researchers concluded that the decision to shoplift often involves a very rational process. While the evidence is far from conclusive, the research strategy shows promise of providing a "window" into the decision-making process. Additional studies on the deterrent component of the rational choice perspective will be considered in the next chapter.

TOWARD A DEVIANCE VULNERABILITY–SHOPLIFTING ATTRACTION THEORETICAL FRAMEWORK

Shoplifting is a complex phenomenon. In attempting to understand it, one must consider the sociocultural context and the creative role that individuals play. Finally, it is important to distinguish between explanations of general predispositions toward deviance and explanations of specific acts of shoplifting. Keeping these assumptions in mind, a framework for analyzing shoplifting will be articulated. Based on the foregoing review of quantitative and qualitative research, the following tentative propositions have been formulated.

First, shoplifting, like many other types of deviance-crime, is more likely to occur when individuals experience social pressures and conditions making them vulnerable to resorting to some type of deviance-crime. *Deviance vulnerability* increases when (1) anomie-strain increases at the societal level, and specifically when it becomes manifested in economic motivations by individuals; (2) individuals perceive that deviance-crime will give them non-economic (sporting and/or psychological) payoffs; (3) the bonds of social control (family, schools, etc.) are weakened; (4) one is surrounded by significant others who are involved in deviance-crime and/or provide neutralizations that justify deviance-crime; and (5) one is labeled a deviant.

Second, individuals vulnerable to becoming deviant are *attracted to choosing a shoplifting option* when (6) significant others provide specific socialization experiences (information on techniques and specific neutralizations) and rewards for shoplifting behavior; (7) initial shoplifting escapades (peer-stimulated, independently initiated, or psychopathology-stimulated) result in rewards-reinforcements (social, economic, psychological); and (8) individuals calculate (from their own or others' experiences) that the rewards of shoplifting exceed the possible risks and costs.

These propositions point to various social conditions and pressures that make individuals more vulnerable to resort to some type of deviance. When a vulnerable individual is exposed to social influences and personal experiences that make shoplifting attractive, there is a greater likelihood that shoplifting will be the type of deviance that is chosen. Future researchers-theorists will have to develop, test, and refine this theoretical formulation.

CONCLUSION

Many major psychiatric/psychological and sociological theories of deviance-crime have been applied to the phenomenon of shoplifting. Macro and micro levels of analysis have been explored. Each theory and level of analysis sheds light on the topic. While the quality of evidence is often less than ideal, the overall sense is that a modest understanding of shoplifting has been attained. Certainly, future work is needed to confirm and refine the propositions presented in the deviance vulnerability–shoplifting attraction formulation.

NOTES

1. Franz Alexander and Hugo Staub (1962) present another detailed and interesting psychoanalytical analysis of a male shoplifter. Numerous sexual and unconscious motivations are imputed to account for this medical doctor's kleptomaniac behavior (e.g., his theft of a microscope is interpreted as a manifestation of his unconscious desire to secretly peep on his mother).

2. Elizabeth Yates (1986) discovered that family problems were frequently evident in shoplifters who had been referred for psychological assessment. Those who were not shoplifting for economic reasons were more likely to exhibit higher levels of depression, but only a few were evaluated as being mentally ill. None of the subjects were considered kleptomaniacs.

3. M. Lindsay Brown (1984) claims that he has encountered only two kleptomaniacs in his security work with over 1,500 apprehended shoplifters.

4. Klemke (1982a) incorporated the labeling perspective into the explanatory analysis of shoplifting. He found a strong relationship between (1) being labeled a troublemaker by teachers and oneself and (2) shoplifting. Whether the labeling occurred prior to or after the shoplifting could not be ascertained by this cross-sectional analysis. Studies by Kraut (1976) and Bales (1982) also present limited supportive data on the labeling perspective. Because of the paucity of evidence, the main discussion of the labeling perspective will be reserved for the next chapter, which looks at the legal handling of the shoplifter.

5. In a similar vein, James W. Coleman's (1989) analysis of white-collar criminals emphasizes the importance of financial self-interest. He points to the key motivation that they want to make a lot of money.

6. The importance of economic and sporting motivations is indirectly supported in a study of college students by Castellano Turner and Sheldon Cashdan (1988). Respondents were asked to identify the reasons why their friends and classmates would shoplift. This projective technique revealed that economic reasons followed by sporting reasons were perceived to be the most important motivations for shoplifting.

7. Thorstein Veblen (1953) has pointed to the tremendous demands placed on individuals by the importance of conspicuous consumption in our society. Orrin Klapp (1969) describes the problems of identity that emerge in a society that encourages a vicious pursuit of status symbols. Edwin Schur (1969) speaks of the crime-encouraging values (excessive materialism, individualism, and competition) of American society's brand of capitalism.

8. Marvin Zuckerman (1978) provides a psychological interpretation of what he calls sensation-seekers.

9. I am indebted to Richard Mitchell for reminding me of this classic essay.

10. Katz constantly emphasizes how deviance is more than a reaction against something negative in one's background (a view that characterizes much sociological theoretical work).

11. Social control theorists have also explored the social world of the peer group. Because there is virtually no explicit research on the quality of bonds with peers and shoplifting, discussion of peer influences will be reserved for the socialization theoretical perspective.

12. It is important to note that students may not be the best source of data to evaluate the impact of schools on their lives. They may not "see" all the "hidden curriculum" or discriminatory decisions that influence their fate in the school setting.

13. It is interesting that the strong relationships between peer support variables and shoplifting are not as strong when individuals are asked to identify why they shoplift. Both Kraut and Klemke found that economic and sporting motivations were more often claimed than peer pressure motivations. Future researchers may need to refine the questions that probe shoplifters' motivations to tap into how peer support may be operating to encourage the economic and sporting motivations that lead to shoplifting behavior.

14. I have also had respondents describe that they had bribed poorly paid security personnel, usually an acquaintance, to look the other way while they were shoplifting.

15. The potent combination of *economic strain* and *criminal neighborhood traditions* was stressed in Richard Cloward and Lloyd Ohlin's (1963) influential "opportunity theory." Other researchers have identified another aspect of opportunity theory. For example, Donald Cressey (1971) and John Clark and Richard Hollinger (1983) have indicated that one must be an insider to commit employee theft. This opportunity factor seems less important for shoplifting, as everyone shops and has access to stores. Perhaps it is useful in explaining why females are more likely to shoplift (because they do more shopping) than to commit robbery or embezzlement.

16. Knowing of my interest in shoplifting, a friend reported the following incident. She recently caught her three-year-old daughter taking a piece of candy from her sock after they had returned from a store. The mother claims that she

has not taught her child how to shoplift and does not know of any other outside influence. One wonders how accurate this child would be if 18 to 20 years in the future, a researcher asks her whether she discovered or was taught how to shoplift.

17. Klemke (1988) outlines a variety of ways in which initial deviance involvement may stimulate more deviance. Of particular interest are "deviance-seeking" quests stimulated by a prior favorable deviance experience.

18. Cressey (1971) and Clark and Hollinger (1983) discovered that many embezzlers and employee thieves articulated neutralizations in justifying their actions.

19. Kraut (1976) and Klemke (1982a) inquired about respondents' motivations for shoplifting. Both discovered that individuals did choose motivations that fit some of the types of neutralizations spelled out by Sykes and Matza.

20. Cornish and Clarke (1986) believe that it also possible to incorporate theories that stress *background* and *macro-sociocultural* factors into the rational choice perspective.

6
DETECTING AND PREVENTING SHOPLIFTING

Some stores hide cameras behind smoked-glass ceiling domes. A number of upscale chains like Marshall Field's in Chicago station store detectives in hollow eight-foot columns with two-way mirrors known as Trojan Horses. At least a dozen major retailers broadcast subliminal messages over store audio systems. The sounds range from police sirens and clanging jail-cell doors to muffled mantras like "Stealing is dishonest."

Dody Tsiantar,
Newsweek (p. 44)

The early-era studies, and a great deal of subsequent research, were devoted to describing and understanding shoplifters and shoplifting. In the early 1970s, however, researchers began to explore a different set of issues. They began to examine the impact of store practices and legal action on shoplifters or prospective shoplifters. The questions raised were (1) How do store security personnel operate, and more specifically, what cues do they utilize when deciding whom to observe and apprehend for shoplifting? (2) How do store personnel decide to prosecute apprehended shoplifters? (3) What impact does being apprehended for shoplifting have on the individual who has been caught? and (4) What can stores and communities do to prevent shoplifting?

The change in focus was due to several factors. First, store decision-makers became more interested in improving their handling of the omnipresent shoplifter problem. Second, researchers were becoming disillusioned with the early-era apprehension studies (there were limited data on limited samples). Third, and probably most important, was the emergence of the labeling perspective as a challenging paradigm in the sociology of deviance literature (Tannenbaum, 1938; Becker, 1963; Wilkins, 1965; Lemert, 1951; Scheff, 1966; Schur, 1971; Thorsell and Klemke, 1972; Hawkins and Tiedeman, 1975). These theorists stimulated numerous studies of agents of control and their practices. They concentrated on assessing the impact of agents of control on the deviant. Therefore, how store officials detected, processed, and impacted shoplifters became an excellent test area to evaluate the value of the labeling perspective.

DETECTING AND APPREHENDING SHOPLIFTERS

How do store security personnel operate, and what cues do store personnel utilize when deciding whom to observe and eventually apprehend for shoplifting? The research and quality of data on this issue are quite weak due to the paucity of good studies of store security personnel and their practices. Cameron (1964), for example, gives only impressionistic insights derived from her observations and interviews with Lakeside Co. security personnel. She describes how they would usually spend more time observing areas of the store that were perceived to be more vulnerable or appealing to shoplifters (e.g., costume jewelry and cosmetic departments instead of furniture departments).

Experienced security personnel often claimed to have developed a "sixth sense" for picking out people who were "likely" suspects. Cameron identified an extensive list of characteristics and cues that served as a "red flag" to the alert Lakeside Co. security officers. Suspicious shoppers and shopper behavior included the following: watching other people more than the merchandise; carrying large purses or shopping bags; wearing bulky clothing or out-of-season clothing; and adolescents or blacks. Security-oriented publications often present trade secrets on how to detect shoplifters (e.g., Edwards, 1970; Faria, 1977; Baumer and Rosenbaum, 1984; and the magazines *Security Management* and *Security World*). Booster Box 10 gives a sample of this type of pragmatic advice.

BOOSTER BOX 10
ADVICE FOR SECURITY PERSONNEL

Security personnel are cautioned about a multitude of potential shoplifting techniques. These include individuals palming small articles and placing them in a pocket, purse, other packages, or bags. Others put on clothing, jewelry, etc. and wear it out of the store or hide it under their clothes. Some shoplifters bring packages, newspapers, umbrellas, baby strollers, etc. into the store that can be used as hiding places. Another technique is to conceal items in another package or item that will be purchased. Price tags may also be switched to give the buyer a real bargain. Some may disguise themselves as a "handicapped," "clerical," "blind" customer, or as someone with a "broken arm" to, hopefully, reduce suspicions of the store personnel.

They are also advised to scrutinize customers who: shop very rapidly and those who linger; hang around back areas of the store and those who stay in crowded areas; are not carrying around or picking up merchandise and those who are carrying around lots of items; are alone and those with other people; act nervous and those who are relaxed; avoid sales personnel and those who pester them. [As should be clear, there are few if any universal cues that security personnel can rely on. Much of this advice is contradictory and/or falls within the realm of normal customer behavior and is therefore of limited value. Perhaps its only utility is that it reinforces the view that security personnel should consider every customer to be a potential shoplifter.]

Source: Material derived from Baumer and Rosenbaum (1984) and Purpura (1984).

In a pioneering article, May (1978) adopts the labeling perspective and sets out to show how agents of control work to "create" shoplifting statistics. Interviews with department store security personnel in Scotland revealed that juveniles were almost universally thought to be prominent suspects for shoplifting. This was particularly the case for juveniles who were lower-class, accompanied by other juveniles,[2] in a store during school hours, known to have delinquent records, and (of course) acting suspiciously. Security officers made sure that they were on duty when school was let out and on Saturdays, because more juveniles would be in the stores. All these practices and biases tended to set in motion a self-fulfilling prophecy and increased the probability of apprehending a disproportionate number of juveniles. This would make security officers look good because they were generating impressive statistics that validated their effectiveness. Therefore, it is surprising that May did not present any apprehension statistics to verify that this was, in fact, taking place. Part of the puzzle might be explained (even though May does not make this explicit) by pursuing the analysis a step further. Because security personnel were selectively targeting juveniles and placing them under close scrutiny (sometimes called shadowing or ghosting), they were likely to be reducing the amount of shoplifting activity that could be committed. Therefore, apprehension statistics can be impacted in various ways by the particular biases and practices of security personnel.

A more extensive study by Murphy (1986) explored the social world of store detectives and their "creation" of shoplifters. He adopted the methodological and theoretical perspective used by May. His investigation covered the full spectrum of retail stores in England. Murphy conducted extensive interviews and ethnographic field observations of store detectives from many different stores. Given what must have been a wealth of data, his analysis is somewhat disappointing.

He does present some interesting anecdotes on how detectives perceive customers/shoplifters. For example, a male acting uncomfortable in the women's lingerie department was not viewed suspiciously until he went into the men's wear section and continued to act furtively. In another case a customer was watched closely because he was putting only expensive items into his shopping cart.

Beyond these types of anecdotes, Murphy mainly confirms the work already reported, that individuals exhibiting atypical customer behavior or fitting the stereotypes of shoplifters received more scrutiny. Children, adolescents, foreigners, and minorities were frequently mentioned by store detectives as being more likely to be shoplifters. This was especially the case when several cues were present, such as a black person with a Rastafarian appearance. Security personnel in a store often developed their own mindset of who should be followed. In one store, for example, Murphy found that black *females* were viewed with special suspicion, while a neighboring store perceived more of a problem with black *males*. Likewise, many idiosyncratic biases influenced the behavior of particular detectives. One particularly disliked Asians, another Middle Easterners, and another always followed women who had bleached their hair peroxide blonde.

Another series of research projects explored the role that *customers* might play in apprehending shoplifters. When a customer sees a person shoplifting, he or she must decide whether to report or ignore the incident. Overall, very few shoplifters are apprehended as a result of customer-initiated action (Klentz and Beaman, 1981). Therefore, these studies are probably more significant as test situations for the labeling perspective or the "bystander" research tradition (Latané and Darley, 1968) than for revealing how shoplifters are typically apprehended. Several projects illustrating this type of research will be summarized briefly.

Darrell Steffensmeier and Robert Terry (1973) and Darrell Steffensmeier and Renée Steffensmeier (1977) designed a field experiment to test the interactionist-labeling perspective. Shoplifting incidents were staged by male/female and hippie/straight research confederates. This was done in front of a store customer. The researchers hypothesized that customers would view the "hippie shoplifter" (compared to a "conventionally dressed shoplifter") and the "male shoplifter" (compared to a "female shoplifter") as being more "deviant," and therefore would be more likely to report them to store employees. Their research did not support the gender hypothesis, but it did confirm that the "hippie shoplifter" was more likely to be reported. They attribute this to the greater stigmatization vulnerability of the hippie appearance. This was dramatically evident in statements made by customers when reporting the incident. One said, "That hippie thing took a package of lunch meat," and another, "That son of a bitch hippie over there just stuffed a banana down his coat" (Steffensmeier and Terry, 1973: 423).

A similar field experiment, based more on the bystander research tradition, was conducted by Donna Gelfand and associates (1973). As in the prior study, shoplifting incidents by a hippie and a conventionally dressed person were staged in front of customers. Even though blatant efforts were made to attract the attention of the 336 shopper-subjects only 28 percent admitted, in subsequent interviews, having seen the staged shoplifting incident. Of those who saw the shoplifting incident, 28 percent reported it to store employees. In contrast to the Steffensmeier and Terry study, hippie shoplifters were not reported more than the conventionally dressed shoplifters. This was surprising because the shoppers did reveal negative attitudes toward hippies in post-experiment interviews.

A more recently staged shoplifting study (a male stealing a bottle of wine) was carried out by Fred Fedler and Bert Pryor (1984). They added some new variations: the size of the "shoplifter" (large vs. small) and the clothing that was worn (well-dressed vs. poorly dressed). The large shoplifter was reported much less frequently. Fedler and Pryor speculated that those observing the shoplifters were less likely to report because of fear of possible retaliation. It is surprising that the well-dressed shoplifter was more likely to be reported than the poorly dressed shoplifter. The investigators discovered in subsequent interviews that the reporters were particularly upset because "If he can afford a suit like that, he doesn't need to steal" (Fedler and Pryor, 1984: 746).

Other interesting variables have been explored in studies of staged shoplifting incidents. One of the more consistent findings of bystander research is that individuals from small towns or rural areas are more likely to intervene in crisis situations than those from large cities. This has also been verified in studies of staged shoplifting events (Gelfand et al., 1973; Bickman and Green, 1977). Less consensus has been obtained on which gender is more likely to report shoplifting by others. Initially, research by Gelfand et al. (1973) reported that males were more likely to report staged shoplifting incidents. Since then, several studies have found that female shoppers were more likely to report a staged incident (Dertke et al., 1974; Bickman and Green, 1977).

Other studies (Bickman, 1975; Bickman and Green, 1977) have attempted to increase the typically low rate of reporting of staged shoplifting incidents. Media campaigns and signs posted in stores encouraged customers to be concerned about shoplifting and solicited citizen involvement in stopping and reporting shoplifting. Individuals exposed to these *impersonal* efforts developed more anti-shoplifting attitudes but did not significantly increase their reporting of staged shoplifting incidents. When more *personal* attempts were included (e.g., attending an anti-shoplifting lecture or having a "confederate shopper" comment that they had also seen someone shoplifting), significantly more staged shoplifting incidents were reported. Overall, these bystander experiments have generated some interesting findings. Nevertheless, they are of limited value because most shoplifters do not come to the attention of store personnel via customer reports.

In summary, surveillance and apprehension practices of store sales and security personnel (or shoppers who volunteer information about shoplifters) cannot be simply characterized as an objective or random process. Shoplifters work at presenting themselves as regular shoppers and at disguising what they are really doing. Many times these "presentations of self and performances," as Erving Goffman (1959) has described, are successfully carried out and the shoplifters are not detected. Consistent with the labeling perspective, security personnel may be affected by self-fulfilling prophecies. Therefore, the shoplifting statistics "created" by security personnel may not accurately reflect shoplifting reality. Security personnel are also frequently diverted from focusing on shoplifters by other job requirements (dealing with customer safety issues or lost children, filling in where sales staff are needed, attempting to detect thefts by employees, etc.).[3] The resulting store apprehension statistics constitute a socially constructed and sometimes distorted picture of who shoplifts. Therefore, store apprehension statistics must be interpreted with caution.

PROSECUTING APPREHENDED SHOPLIFTERS

While studies of store records are limited in what they can tell us about shoplifters, they may be an excellent source of data for revealing how store personnel decide to prosecute apprehended shoplifters.[4] Some of the best research on shoplifting has been devoted to this issue. Cameron (1964) provides the first sketchy look at how apprehended shoplifters are processed. She discovered that shoplifters who were perceived to be professionals (boosters) were almost always formally charged. The remainder of her analysis of how Lakeside Co. decided to prosecute focused on the race of the apprehended suspect. She discovered that while 58 percent of the blacks apprehended at Lakeside Co.

were formally prosecuted, only 10.9 percent of the whites were so
charged. A similar over-representation of black females was observed
when she looked at court records for Chicago. While apprehended shoplifters who had taken more expensive items were generally more likely
to be prosecuted by Lakeside Co., she found that blacks who were
formally charged had taken less expensive merchandise than the whites.
This led her to conclude that the official statistics on racial patterns of
shoplifting were misleading due to discrimination by store personnel.
A smaller racial prosecution bias against blacks was also noted in Gerald
Robin's (1963) study of Philadelphia department stores. Both these studies suggest that race was a significant factor in determining who received
a legal shoplifting label in the pre–civil rights era.

The early studies were followed by a series of more sophisticated
statistical analyses of factors affecting the decision to prosecute or release
an apprehended shoplifter. Usually, these studies were designed to test
the labeling perspective. Cohen and Stark (1974), for example, looked
at what happened to individuals apprehended for shoplifting in a large
California department store. They evaluated the impact of race, sex, age,
social class, the amount of money the person carried, whether a purchase
was made, and the dollar value of the stolen merchandise on the eventual
decision to release or prosecute the shoplifter. After conducting a series
of statistical analyses, they concluded that the value of the stolen merchandise (over $30 being a more serious offense) was the strongest pre-
dictor of prosecution. They also found that those who were unemployed
were more likely to be prosecuted. Because seriousness of offense was
the most important determinant, and age, sex, and race biases were not
evident, they claimed that their analysis challenged the efficacy of the
labeling perspective. More specifically, the absence of a racial bias con-
flicted with Cameron's early findings.

This study was followed by similar analyses conducted by other investigators. Hindelang (1974) analyzed over 6,000 cases of apprehended
supermarket shoplifters. His analysis focused on age, sex, race, types
of items stolen, and the value of items stolen (over $1.90). Employing
a predictive attribute analysis (PAA) statistical approach, he concluded
that age, sex, and race were at best only slightly related to the decision
to refer the apprehended shoplifter to the police. As in the earlier studies,
the dollar value of the item stolen was very significant in predicting
referral to the police (only 13% of the under-$1.90 value shoplifters were
referred, compared to 40% of those taking merchandise worth more
than $1.90). This difference would probably have been even larger had
a greater dollar value been selected as the cutting point. Focusing on
supermarkets, Hindelang also noted a more specialized finding: that the
type of item taken affected a person's chances of being released or referred to the police. The PAA statistics showed that stealing liquor or

cigarettes increased the likelihood of being referred. Hindelang also concluded that his data gave very little support for the labeling perspective.

A replication of this study was conducted by Lundman (1978) on data
from a midwestern department store. He initially noted that those who
had taken more expensive items were much more likely to be referred
to the police. He then conducted a PAA analysis to explore the importance of age, sex, and race on the referral decision. In contrast to the
two prior studies, age (being over 18 years old) and race (being non-
white) significantly increased the likelihood of being referred to the
police. This held even when the dollar value of the stolen item was
controlled.

Additional insight on security decision making is found in Murphy's
(1986) study. He emphasizes that an arrest was more likely to be made
when the security officer had strong evidence to back up legal action.
If, for example, more than one item was observed being taken, there
was a greater likelihood of arrest. Suspects who resisted or ran when
being detained, denied wrongdoing, or showed no remorse were more
likely to be arrested.[5] Finally, large stores were more likely to prosecute
than smaller stores who had fewer personnel to devote to these matters.

The issue has also been explored by Audrey Feuerverger and Clifford
Shearing (1982) with a very different research strategy. They developed
typewritten descriptions of hypothetical shoplifting cases. Seven variables (sex, age, race, dollar value, admission of offense, and the attitude
and appearance of the offender) were systematically varied in the 192
hypothetical cases. Booster Box 11 shows one of these cases.

BOOSTER BOX 11
HYPOTHETICAL CASE A

You apprehend a 68-year-old white male after he leaves the store
without paying for a package of batteries that you saw him conceal on his person. The batteries are valued at $3.10. The man
looks neat and clean and is well dressed. Throughout the interview he is respectful and agreeable toward you. He admits that
he intentionally stole the batteries and agrees to sign a statement
to that effect.

Source: Audrey Feuerverger and Clifford D. Shearing. 1982. "An Analysis of the
Prosecution of Shoplifters." *Criminology* 20(August): 277.

Twenty security personnel from four large department stores were selected as research subjects. Each respondent read nine or ten of the

hypothetical cases and then indicated whether he or she would prosecute each "offender."

Analysis revealed that the best predictor of the decision to prosecute was stealing an item valued over $20. Offenders who denied committing the act were also very likely to be prosecuted to protect the security investigator from being sued for false arrest. Young (under age 16) and elderly (over age 60) shoplifters were especially likely to be treated with leniency and not be prosecuted. Surprisingly, well-dressed shoplifters were more likely to be prosecuted than poorly dressed ones. Follow-up interviews revealed very little sympathy for shoplifters who were perceived as being able to afford the stolen items. Finally, race and gender did not appear to affect the decision to prosecute. It should be recalled that the respondents were reporting how they "would" deal with a particular case, not how they had "actually" performed in real life. Even though this introduces some distortion from their real behavior, it is still useful in revealing what they think they would do. Furthermore, most of the findings were similar to those uncovered in the review of studies of real-life decisions.

Kenneth Adams and Charles Cutshall (1984) studied how shoplifters were dealt with after they had been arrested by the police.[6] They specifically analyzed whether the prosecutor in the criminal justice system proceeded or dismissed (nolle prosequi) the case. Their analysis of 745 cases from the District of Columbia revealed that arrested shoplifters were most likely to have their cases dismissed when they had no, or only one, prior arrest (legal factors). Albeit less predictive, gender and race (extralegal factors) were also related to the decision to dismiss. Specifically, females and whites were more likely to have their cases dismissed. Instead of invoking a blatant racism or sexism interpretation, the researchers speculate that district attorneys see many more blacks or males being arrested. Therefore, the prosecutors perceive that they pose a greater threat to the community and require more severe sanctions.

Finally, Melissa Davis et al. (1991) conducted an interesting analysis of how a large mall store handled apprehended shoplifters. The research was focused on ascertaining why some shoplifters were arrested while others were put into a civil recovery process. This revealed that shoplifters were more likely to be arrested when: they had taken expensive items, they resisted being apprehended, they had no local address, and they lived in less affluent neighborhoods. The researchers concluded that the more affluent shoplifters were sent through the civil recovery process because they would be more likely to pay the civil penalty while the less affluent were sent into the criminal justice system.

As the various studies attest, many factors can influence the decisions on how to deal with an apprehended shoplifter. Generally, legalistic factors (like seriousness of offense and prior arrest record) seem to be more important today than the extralegal factors. For example, blatant racist biases are less evident today than in Cameron's Chicago data. It is probably true that there remains tremendous variability from store to store on how objectively security personnel deal with apprehended shoplifters.

DOES APPREHENSION AMPLIFY OR TERMINATE SHOPLIFTING?

A central tenet of the labeling perspective is that being labeled a deviant could have the unintended effect of increasing the amount of future deviance committed by that person. Tannenbaum (1938) originally expressed concern that legal entanglements might transform the novice troublemaker into a confirmed delinquent. This idea was also stressed by Lemert (1967), who saw labeling experiences as being instrumental in pushing individuals from primary deviance (initial and exploratory deviance) to secondary deviance (where deviance becomes a significant part of one's self because of labeling). Scheff (1966) elaborated that labeling often results in (1) other people expecting the labeled deviant to commit more deviance; (2) roadblocks being placed in the path of returning to conforming behavior; (3) rewards for continuing deviance; and (4) acceptance of a deviant identity by the labeled person. Thus, labeling theorists have stressed that agents of control may, ironically, increase the deviance that they are avowedly attempting to suppress. This prediction of escalating involvement in deviance has been termed the apprehension-deviance amplification hypothesis by Klemke (1978a).

Deterrence theorists have challenged these ideas. They claim that social control efforts (labeling experiences) and the threat of sanctions can reduce subsequent deviance (Chambliss, 1984; Tittle, 1969; Tittle and Rowe, 1973; Van Den Hagg, 1975). The issue has been referred to in the literature as *specific deterrence*. Deterrence theorists argue that the greater the certainty and severity of punishment (i.e., labeling), the greater the reduction in future deviance by the individual subjected to punishment. Klemke (1978a) has called this the apprehension-deviance termination hypothesis. The tremendous importance of these ideas to policymakers and social scientists has stimulated a great deal of research. Sherman (1990) reviewed the literature on randomized experiments designed to shed light on this issue. Unfortunately, he discovered conflicting evidence on the effects of sanctions. Some studies reported that recidivism was reduced, in others recidivism was increased, and still others showed no significant difference.

Likewise, many of my own interview respondents have highlighted the importance of being caught. Typically, more individuals refer to it as an embarrassing experience and claim it was the reason why they stopped shoplifting. On the other hand, others claim that being caught shoplifting taught them that they (1) should not be so careless in the future; (2) could talk their way out of their predicament; (3) only had to endure a chastising lecture; or (4) just received a "hand slap" from the legal authorities. Therefore, these individuals continued to shoplift.

A review of the quantitative shoplifting research addresses the question: What impact does being apprehended for shoplifting have on the individual who has been caught? As before, Cameron (1964) presents the first analysis of this issue. She searched for the names of individuals apprehended at the Lakeside Co. department store in the security records of ten other major stores and the city police arrest records. Only 2 percent of the female and 6 percent of the male Lakeside Co. snitches were discovered as repeat shoplifters. The few Lakeside Co. shoplifters who were considered to be boosters were more likely to have repeated apprehensions for shoplifting. Cameron reasoned that snitches did not think of themselves as thieves prior to being apprehended. Therefore, an apprehension (labeling) experience forced them to reevaluate their behavior. Most decided that they did not want to be a thief and stopped shoplifting. Of course, an alternate interpretation could be that apprehended shoplifters learned from their prior mistake and took more precautions to avoid a future apprehension.

A subsequent study by Cohen and Stark (1974) found very few repeaters (only 3 out of 371 apprehended supermarket shoplifters) in the files of a major private security company serving the area of their study. They also concluded that virtually no one continues to shoplift after being apprehended. Many writers have taken these studies as strong evidence supporting the apprehension-deviance termination hypothesis.

This conclusion has been questioned because of the methodological shortcomings of the studies (Klemke, 1978a). The limitations are as follows: (1) as only records of apprehended shoplifters were searched, any shoplifting that did not result in an apprehension could not be detected; (2) typically, only a few of the many possible store records were searched for repeaters; and (3) many apprehended shoplifters are not referred to the police and therefore would not show up in the police records searched by Cameron. Overall, there are serious under-reporting biases in these studies. To avoid these problems, Klemke (1978b) utilized a self-report methodology. He asked youth whether they had ever been arrested for shoplifting, how the apprehension was handled (if police were called), and whether they had shoplifted after they were apprehended. This strategy constitutes a more thorough test of the apprehension-deviance amplification versus the apprehension-deviance termination hypothesis.

Table 6.1
Shoplifting Behavior After Being Apprehended by Store Personnel, by Sex
(in percentages)

	Times shoplifted after apprehension by store personnel:			
Sex	Never	1-4	5+	N
Males	61	26	13	(117)
Females	60	18	22	(72)
Total	60	24	16	(189)

Source: Adapted from Table 1 in Lloyd W. Klemke (1978), "Does Apprehension for Shoplifting Amplify or Terminate Shoplifting Activity?" (*Law and Society Review*
12(Spring): 396).

From this research, Klemke found that 25 percent of the youth who had shoplifted reported having been apprehended by store personnel.[7] Table 6.1 reveals that 40 percent of these youth reported that they continued to shoplift after having been apprehended by store personnel. Additional data (not shown) revealed that 54 percent of the youth apprehended by parents reported that they had shoplifted after this informal labeling experience. Likewise, recent shoplifting (during the last eight months; data not shown) was reported by 36 percent of the shoplifting respondents who had never been apprehended by store personnel, 39 percent of those apprehended once, and 46 percent of those apprehended two or more times. This shows that many of the apprehended youth had not terminated their shoplifting activity.

Even though they predict opposite outcomes, labeling and deterrence theorists both emphasize the importance of the police. Therefore, Klemke analyzed subsequent shoplifting behavior when store personnel did or did not call the police. The data revealed that youth who were apprehended for shoplifting and who experienced police intervention (a stronger labeling experience) were slightly more likely to continue shoplifting (48%) than those who did not experience police intervention (40%).

These statistics show that much larger percentages of individuals continue to shoplift after being apprehended than were reported by Cameron (6% and lower) and by Cohen and Stark (less than 1%). While none of the relationships are very strong, all are in the direction predicted by the apprehension-deviance amplification hypothesis. Therefore, they provide modest support for the labeling theoretical perspective.

In an effort to upgrade the quality of evidence on this issue, a randomized experiment was designed by Lawrence Sherman and Patrick Gartin (1986) and the Police Foundation. They were primarily interested in finding out whether arresting or releasing apprehended shoplifters would have any impact on recidivism rates. In cooperation with nine branches of a Detroit department store, 1,595 apprehended shoplifters were randomly assigned to be either arrested or released. Data were collected on the offender and what had transpired during the apprehension (e.g., if the offender resisted). State and local police arrest records were obtained for a six-month period after the shoplifting apprehension. Inevitably, implementation of the experimental design encountered some problems. There was some slippage in faithfully carrying out the random assignment, but analysis revealed that it did not appreciably alter the results. There were also minor disparities in the recidivism statistics of Sherman and Gartin's report (1986) and the Police Foundation report of the results (Williams et al., 1987).

Sherman and Gartin analyzed what they considered to be the best quality data. They found that 5.7 percent of the *arrested shoplifters* were rearrested for shoplifting and 5.9 percent of the *released shoplifters* were rearrested in the six-month period after their apprehension. These figures are quite large considering that they cover a short time period and do not include self-reports of shoplifting behavior or store apprehensions. The researchers initially concluded that being arrested did not add any significant deterrent effect to the apprehension experience.

However, an analysis for interaction effects turned up several qualifications to the main pattern. Several crude indicators of "underclass" status (sloppy attire and race) were obtained by the researchers. Sloppy dressers and blacks who were arrested were less likely to recidivate than those who were released. On the other hand, "mainstream" types of apprehended shoplifters (i.e., those who were better educated, females, employed adults, and whites) who were arrested were more likely to recidivate than those who were not.[8] These findings led Sherman and Gartin to conclude that there are important differences in the effects of sanctions on the recidivism of different types of people.[9] Overall, their study provides a model methodology and challenging findings for theorists and policymakers. One hopes that others will replicate and continue to refine this research approach.

So far, the labeling and deterrence advocates have argued that the negative experience of being punished (e.g., apprehended, arrested, fined, placed on probation) may either increase or decrease future deviance. In some communities, an apprehended shoplifter may be subjected to treatment programs designed to reduce future shoplifting behavior (Schwartz and Wood, 1991). These more positive approaches may still be viewed as punishment by involuntary subjects and by labeling theorists. Still, they constitute a different strategy that should be considered apart from traditional punishment approaches.

One example of this type of program is the educational rehabilitation program, Shoplifters Anonymous. It is currently promoted by Peter D. Berlin.[10] For a small fee per client, court systems may require that convicted shoplifters work through a set of lessons (at home or in a classroom setting). The lessons are designed to (1) undermine justifications for shoplifting (consistent with the neutralization theory); (2) sensitize shoplifters to the costs and stigma resulting from shoplifting (consistent with the rational choice and labeling theory); and (3) develop a personal plan to stop shoplifting. Successful completion may enable the shoplifter to have his or her arrest record expunged. Only professional shoplifters are excluded from the program. Program literature claims a surprisingly low 1.3 percent recidivism rate but does not provide the basis for the figure. An independent evaluation should be made of this program.

Another program for convicted shoplifters is reported by Anita Sue Kolman and Claudia Wasserman (1991). They describe the Theft Program for Women run by the Ramsey County Community Corrections Department in Minnesota and the Wilder Foundation. Women with little or no criminal history are eligible for this program. It has much the same rationale and focus as the Shoplifters Anonymous program, but it occurs in seven weekly small-group counseling sessions. The authors' limited evaluation of 164 consecutive participants revealed primarily positive changes. Participants felt that they had gained a better understanding of why they shoplifted. Furthermore, 94 percent had no convictions for any criminal activity in the year after completing the program. Unfortunately, no self-report data were obtained on their criminal behavior.

David Royse and Steven Buck (1991) evaluated a diversion program for shoplifters. Only individuals with no prior shoplifting arrests were given the option of participating in the program. Participants were required to complete eight hours of a psycho-educational group experience and to fulfill 60 hours of community service. When they had successfully completed these obligations, the shoplifting charge was removed from their records. Only 4 percent of those completing the program were rearrested for shoplifting in the one year follow-up period compared to about 25 percent for various comparison groups. The authors point to the strong possibility that the individuals who chose to participate probably eliminated many "poor risk" candidates from the program. A similar program (minus the community service component) was designed for youth (Winfree et al., 1989). Less than 3 percent of both participants and non-participants were rearrested for shoplifting during the 8- to 24-month follow-up period. Unlike Royse and Buck, Winfree and his colleagues obtained arrest statistics for other types of criminal offenses. Program participants had slightly fewer other arrests than did non-participants.

The positive results obtained on almost all of these programs are encouraging even though they exclude the tougher cases. However, the findings need to be confirmed by better quality evaluation research conducted by independent researchers. Research also needs to be done on other treatment-diversion programs (like the Victim Offender Reconciliation Program) that handle many shoplifters.

INTRODUCTION TO DETERRING AND PREVENTING SHOPLIFTING

How do stores and communities attempt to reduce shoplifting behavior? This question expands the scope of the analysis to the issues of general deterrence and prevention. In contrast to specific deterrence, general deterrence strategies and practices target potential shoplifters in the general public. It is argued that making it more difficult to shoplift, or increasing the risks and penalties for shoplifting, will reduce the number of people who shoplift. These punitive approaches may be complemented by positive information-educational approaches to prevention.

More manpower and print has been devoted to dealing with shoplifters than to understanding their deviance. Complementing the in-store security forces and efforts are numerous security publications and organizations that give advice on how to reduce shoplifting losses. This gives the appearance of a concerted war against shoplifting (Albanese, 1984). In reality, however, shoplifting is often not a high priority problem. This is because retailers, particularly large stores, are able to compensate for shoplifting losses (and other types of shrinkage) through price increases. Therefore, retail decision-makers are often reluctant to adopt security technology or practices that (1) might cut into sales; (2) can be costly (in dollars, customer goodwill (Guffey et al., 1979) and/or employee time); and (3) may be only marginally effective in reducing shoplifting.

As developed in Chapter 5, sociological theories identify many social factors associated with shoplifting. Awareness of this has clouded optimism that shoplifting can be significantly reduced because many of these factors are beyond the control of the retail community (Currie, 1985; Walker, 1985). Retailers can, at best, only indirectly alter the associational patterns, economic situation of the general public, drug subculture practices, quality of family life, and so forth in the larger society that are related to shoplifting behavior. This leads to the pessimistic conclusion that *anti-shoplifting efforts by the retain community will not result in dramatic overall reductions in shoplifting activity*.

On the other hand, the rational choice and deterrence theoretical proponents suggest a limited but more optimistic outlook. These theorists acknowledge that retailers can (1) influence the perceptions of how risky it is to attempt to shoplift, and (2) design, "police," and control the interiors of their own business establishments in ways that will increase the difficulty of shoplifting. Accomplishing such goals should produce a reduction of shoplifting activity.

With this general introduction to the limits and possibilities of reducing shoplifting, we will now look more closely at two specific approaches. The first are primarily in-store programs; the second are educational and informational approaches that typically range beyond the confines of a store.

IN-STORE PREVENTION DEVICES AND STRATEGIES

If retailers were not primarily concerned with increasing sales and maintaining positive customer attitudes, it would not be too difficult to design a relatively shoplift-proof store. In fact, many jewelry stores already present a viable high-security model. The trend in the retail community has been to move in the opposite direction. The low-security stores (self-service, combining high access to merchandise and minimal sales staff) have become more popular.[11] These customer-friendly stores have a significantly higher sales volume that, it is hoped, will more than offset the predictably higher shoplifting losses.

A number of key issues confront individuals in charge of designing and implementing store security. Which types of technology and programs will be most effective in reducing shoplifting? How much weight should be placed on using real people compared to technological (monitoring and security devices) approaches? It is beyond the scope of this book to cover all possible approaches and strategies. The intent is to cover some of the major tactics. Where possible, the pros and cons of the different approaches will be developed. Security experts and the limited evaluation research literature will be the main sources of information.[12]

A great deal of ingenuity has been shown in devising strategies to foil the prospective shoplifter (Faria, 1977; Farrell, 1985; Davis et al., 1991). Just as there are numerous and ingenious ways of shoplifting, there are equally numerous and ingenious ways of discouraging shoplifting. Basically, they include attempts to (1) make it more difficult to take items; and/or (2) foster the perception that shoplifting would be too risky. The more successful a store is in accomplishing either of these two general goals, the larger the reductions in shoplifting losses it should experience.

Almost all types of shoplifting could be reduced by restricting access to merchandise or creating the impression that the item has been theft-protected. Moore's impulse-occasional shoplifters would be most likely affected by these tactics. Similarly, Cameron (1964) has speculated that snitches are more likely to be deterred than the more resourceful boosters. Finally, Carroll and Weaver (1986) conducted a field study of what "shoplifters are thinking." They concluded that novice shoplifters are "sheeplike" and can be deterred by almost anything (e.g., sales personnel looking at them or security cameras), but that experienced shoplifters are more like "wolves" who adjust their strategies to overcome security personnel or technological devices.

Innumerable simple techniques and products can provide considerable protection against shoplifting. The literature contains many different panaceas that have been touted as solutions to the shoplifting problem. Abelson's (1989b) historical analysis reveals how the development of glass showcases and glass windows revolutionized early department stores. They allowed merchandise to be attractively and enticingly displayed to the customer and yet be protected from the nimble fingers of the shoplifter. Other elementary technological approaches use various "target-hardening" strategies such as placing locking devices on expensive merchandise and putting small, attractive items (e.g., cassette tapes, cosmetics) into larger packages that are more difficult to conceal. The layout of the store and arrangement of displays and checkout counters can either enhance or complicate store security efforts. Simply placing more expensive merchandise away from the exits can reduce incidents of "snatch and run" shoplifting.

More sophisticated electronic article surveillance (EAS) technology has been developed to protect expensive items. While there are different types of EAS, all result in an alarm going off if an item is taken out of the store without being deactivated. The systems are costly to purchase and maintain. To reduce the expense of this approach, "dummy" EAS tags may be visibly placed on merchandise to create the impression that it is protected.

Besides making it more difficult to take items, it is possible to foster the perception that shoplifting is too risky. A standard crime prevention strategy is to increase the number or visibility of "guardians" who are charged with monitoring and protecting vulnerable targets. This can be accomplished by increasing the number of guardians or by using technological devices. It is frequently claimed that alert and well-trained sales staff and security officers provide the best protection against shoplifting. Very little evidence, besides the opinion of experienced security personnel, backs up this assertion (Baumer and Rosenbaum, 1984).[13]

Aiding and complementing these human guardians are various technological devices. Some stores use controversial subliminal messages (such as "Thou shalt not steal" and the sound of police sirens) in their music systems (Baumer and Rosenbaum, 1984). Customers/shoplifters can be "watched" by convex mirrors, two-way mirrors, closed-circuit television (CCTV) monitors, and EAS systems, and from hidden observation locations (e.g., Trojan Horses). One of the latest innovations is a mannequin called Anne Droid. It contains a miniaturized camera behind its glass eyes to observe unsuspecting shoplifters (Sloane, 1991). Even if these devices are not constantly monitored or are illusory (e.g., fake CCTV cameras), they may still intimidate and deter some potential shoplifters (Schlueter et al., 1989). Some security experts feel that when a store goes "hi-tech," store personnel may no longer feel that they have to be as vigilant and, ironically, shoplifting becomes easier.

Farrell (1985) takes one of the strongest stands that stores should mount a thorough (in-store and in the community) and tough anti-shoplifting program. She explicitly advises that customers and the public be constantly warned of the program by signs and posters (e.g., "Shoplifters—All Eyes Are On You," and random in-store announcements that "security should report to specific departments"). Stores have reportedly hired actors to stage random "shoplifting arrest incidents" to convey to potential shoplifters that it is a store to avoid (*Business Week*, 1979). Regrettably, there is very limited evaluation research to assess the deterrence power of these many different strategies.

Klemke's (1978a) high school students were asked how much "mirrors, cameras, or signs to warn people from taking items without paying for them" scared people from taking things. Findings for the total sample showed the following pattern: 12.6 percent felt that the devices "scare most people," 50 percent that they "scare some people," 31.9 percent that they "only scare a few people," and 5.5 percent that they "do not scare anybody." This pattern remained virtually unchanged for youth who had shoplifted and for youth who had been caught shoplifting. The high school students were also asked to identify stores that "make the most effort to discourage and catch shoplifters." Many of the students (almost 60%) were able to identify one to three specific "tough" stores. Being aware that a store is tough on shoplifters does not guarantee that individuals will avoid shoplifting there. In fact, about 25 percent of those identifying tough stores had recently shoplifted in one. Unfortunately, the question was not phrased to sort out those who had shoplifted and been caught, leading them to consider the store a tough store. Refining this approach should be valuable for future rational choice and deterrence theorists. Likewise, the retail community should be very interested in promoting such research, particularly when a store wants to assess whether a "get tough" campaign is actually changing the public's perceptions and reducing shoplifting.

Every in-store anti-shoplifting strategy or technological device has advantages and disadvantages. It is beyond the scope of this analysis to critique each approach. However, it is important to explore one potential limitation that they all share. *As long as only some stores adopt stronger in-store anti-shoplifting approaches, one can expect that a significant amount of the shoplifting "prevented" in one store will simply be relocated to more vulnerable neighboring stores.* This has been called a displacement effect. Because of the difficulty of documenting the phenomenon, there do not appear to be any studies of how much shoplifting may be displaced from one store to another.

Reviewing the general deviance literature on displacement effects helps to shed some light on this topic. For example, research on police crackdowns of street drug sales have led to contradictory conclusions. Some have claimed that crackdowns have resulted in large overall reductions in drug crimes, while others report that drug sales have simply relocated to "safer" areas (Chaiken, 1988). Several reviews of the evaluation literature aimed at assessing displacement effects have concluded that *at least some crime can be eliminated by specific target-hardening crime prevention efforts* (Cornish and Clarke, 1986; Lab, 1988; Sherman, 1990). Most of these analysts are working from the rational choice theoretical perspective. Therefore, when a potential offender perceives that the risks of shoplifting have increased in one store, she or he must decide whether to still do it there (taking appropriate countermeasures); go to a safer store to shoplift (displacement response); or refrain from shoplifting. An in-depth interview study of how these calculations and actions unfold in the real world would be a valuable contribution to the shoplifting literature. Lab (1988) cites research suggesting that more active offenders are more likely to seek out safer crime targets (i.e., make wiser decisions) than are situational-impulse offenders. Security personnel also generally believe that non-professional shoplifters are more likely to be intimidated by intensified security efforts.

EDUCATIONAL AND INFORMATIONAL PREVENTION STRATEGIES

Many communities and retail organizations have attempted to inform the public about the shoplifting problem and to create anti-shoplifting attitudes. Generally, these take the form of publicity campaigns designed to reduce shoplifting. They may take place within a store or be coordinated in a community media campaign. At the store level there have been programs to post sign warning that "Shoplifting is a Crime" or informing customers of the presence of various security measures ("Smile, you're on TV"). This simple and inexpensive strategy has received mixed evaluations. M. Patrick McNees et al. (1976) conducted two experiments. They found that anti-shoplifting signs did reduce the number of items being taken. The time frame for the study was only weeks; therefore, a long-term impact was not ascertained. Steven Thurber and Mark Snow (1980) conducted a similar study. They concluded that posting "Everyone Pays for Shoplifting" signs above the cigarette carton display actually *prompted* an increase in the theft of cigarettes. While more definitive research is certainly needed, one should not expect too much or a lasting impact from such a superficial change tactic.

More extensive community campaigns to prevent shoplifting have utilized a variety of techniques to increase public awareness of the seriousness of shoplifting, encourage citizen reporting of shoplifting, and increase awareness of the negative consequences of being apprehended for shoplifting. Baumer and Rosenbaum (1984) present a very good descriptive summary of these types of programs. They highlight campaigns that target schools, businesses, and cities or states. Posters, pamphlets, classes, advertisements, and public service announcements are frequently used to get the message to the public. A campaign that used most of these approaches was evaluated by Chok Hiew (1981). He looked at Operation S.O.S. (Stop Our Shoplifting), which took place in a Canadian community. Extensive community participation (schools, stores, and media) was orchestrated during the early months of the project. Hiew reported reductions in shoplifting apprehensions and prosecutions after the S.O.S. campaign. Presumably, these changes were due to the campaign and not because of changes in store security personnel behavior.

Generally, only weak evaluation research has been done on these types of programs. The most extensive critical review has been done by Vincent Sacco (1985). He concludes that these programs are most likely to change attitudes (to see shoplifting as a more serious problem) but are less likely to change behavior. There are many reasons why the campaigns have only a limited impact. The most important being that they are very superficial; only conducted for a short time period; and presented through impersonal sources (e.g., mass media, posters) and by authority figures (teachers, police). Of course, they do not alter any of the psychological or sociological causes of shoplifting.

Another complication may undermine this type of strategy. Alerting the public to the problem of shoplifting may actually stimulate shoplifting among some individuals who had not been considering it. There is very little evidence to support this for anti-shoplifting campaigns, except the Thurber and Snow study cited earlier. Research on a different type of deviance, conducted by Phillips (1974), revealed that a small number of suicides may be stimulated by a nationally publicized suicide. A similar boomerang effect could occur during an anti-shoplifting campaign.

OVERVIEW

This chapter has reviewed studies on how shoplifters and security personnel interact, impact, and attempt to influence each other. Numerous insights and lessons are instructive to social scientists. Many of the research and theoretical questions central to the labeling and deterrence literature structured the analysis. Tentative findings were given on how store security personnel detect, apprehend, process, and attempt to deter shoplifting. This information should be useful to security personnel and the retail community. Clearly, there are no indications that the war against shoplifting will produce a quick victory over shoplifters. A more likely scenario is that there will be continuing competition between retailers and customer-shoplifters, with each side claiming minor conquests and victories.

NOTES

1. A customer coming into a store in winter without a coat may be viewed as a shoplifting candidate who might attempt to wear a stolen coat out of the store.

2. One of my respondents stated that she always invited her mother to go shopping with her when she was going to shoplift. The unsuspecting mother was used to reduce suspicion among store personnel that the young girl might be a potential shoplifter.

3. William Bolen (1988) identifies ten different security issues that an effective store security system should consider. In addition, security personnel in many stores are expected to help out in sales and may have management responsibilities that dilute their potential effectiveness.

4. Research by French et al. (1984) revealed considerable variability in prosecution rates for different stores.

5. Robert Emerson (1991) reports that shoplifting juveniles were more likely to be referred to the juvenile court when they were uncooperative toward store detectives.

6. Murphy (1986) also describes how shoplifters are legally dealt with in England.

7. In a study of Seattle youth, Hindelang et al. (1981) discovered that 32.8 percent of white males, 29.3 percent of black males, 23.8 percent of white females, and 23.8 percent of black females admitted to having been caught by store personnel. Kraut (1976) found that only 16 percent of his college student shoplifters reported having been caught. (Are college-bound youth more proficient thieves?) Unfortunately, these studies did not pursue how much the respondents shoplifted after being apprehended.

8. The analysts suggest that mainstream types may have received more lenient handling and punishments, and therefore they were willing to risk shoplifting again.

9. Smith and Gartin (1989) examined the impact of being arrested on future

criminal activity for a cohort of males in Racine, Wisconsin. They discovered that an arrest was more likely to *terminate* criminal careers for novice offenders and that experienced offenders were likely to *reduce* offending after an arrest.

10. More information on this program can be obtained from Shoplifters Anonymous, 380 North Broadway, Suite 206, Jericho, New York 11753–9838.

11. Lawrence E. Cohen and Marcus Felson (1979) present some crude trend data showing that shoplifting has increased as the number of sales personnel (guardians of the merchandise) has been reduced.

12. A major obstacle to conducting evaluation research on shoplifting prevention programs has been the difficulty of pinpointing and validating how much of the shrinkage loss is due to shoplifting.

13. One modest confirmation of this idea comes from my own convenience sample of college student shoplifters (mentioned in Chapter 1). Data from this preliminary study showed that 53 percent of the shoplifters "worry a great deal" about "sales clerks and security officers catching them," but that only 31 percent were as concerned about "video cameras, electronic tags, mirrors, etc."

7

OVERVIEW

Almost 30 years ago, Mary Owen Cameron produced the first extensive sociological study of shoplifting. The goal of this book was to update Cameron's effort by critically reviewing the research and theoretical work that has been accumulating on the topic. Initially, I naively intended to generate a book that provided "everything you ever wanted to know about shoplifting." Now, many months later and considerably more humble, I consider my efforts to constitute a very good starting point for future researchers and theorists.

My analysis addressed the three major concerns that pervade the sociology of deviance literature. Therefore, I expended a great deal of energy to develop (1) descriptions of shoplifting, (2) explanations of shoplifting, and (3) an analysis of how retailers deal with shoplifting.

Generally speaking, good descriptive research on who shoplifts and how shoplifting occurs has been accumulating. Many clear patterns have been identified, and others at least specify tentative benchmarks that future research can clarify. A number of deficiencies and gaps in our knowledge, particularly for adult, female, and middle-class shoplifting, remain as special challenges for future researchers.

Explanations of shoplifting are currently at a rudimentary level of development. Existing research on shoplifting provides only scattered and limited tests of traditional explanations of deviance. A critical review of the research-theoretical literature revealed that many sociological theories of deviance-crime do offer considerable insight into why shoplifting occurs. A deviance vulnerability–shoplifting attraction theoretical framework was derived from the theoretical review. This attempt at theoretical integration is offered here as a preliminary statement. I hope it will serve as a stimulus that can and will be sharpened and improved. At any rate, additional efforts to develop a theory of shoplifting should be encouraged.

Finally, retailers' quest for solutions to the shoplifting problem appears to be a continuing and frustrating challenge. Too many factors in our society continue to make shoplifting an easy and rewarding form of deviance. Even though retailers could do much more to protect their merchandise (ignoring displacement effects), they are often reluctant to give security their highest priority. This is because many security measures are expensive, and retailers are also concerned that sales will decline in a high-security store.

Therefore, one can confidently assert that shoplifting will continue to be a popular budget-stretching type of deviance; plague retailers; frustrate security personnel; and provide an enticing and tantalizing phenomenon for sociologists. I hope this book will stimulate and facilitate the research and theoretical work of the next generation of students of shoplifting.

REFERENCES

Abelson, Elaine S. 1989a. "The Invention of Kleptomania." *Signs: Journal of Women in Culture and Society* 15(1): 123–43.

———. 1989b. *When Ladies Go A-Thieving: Middle Class Shoplifters in the Victorian Department Store*. New York: Oxford University Press.

Adams, Kenneth, and Charles R. Cutshall. 1984. "Refusing to Prosecute Minor Offenses: The Relative Influence of Legal and Extralegal Factors." *Justice Quarterly* 4(4): 595–609.

Adler, Freda. 1975. *Sisters in Crime: The Rise of the New Female Criminal*. New York: McGraw-Hill.

Agnew, Robert. 1983. "Goal Achievement and Delinquency." *Sociology and Social Research* 68(4): 435–51.

———. 1990. "The Origin of Delinquent Events: An Examination of Offender Accounts." *Journal of Research in Crime and Delinquency* 27 (August): 267–94.

Agnew, Robert, and Ardith A. R. Peters. 1986. "The Techniques of Neutralization: An Analysis of Predisposing and Situational Factors." *Criminal Justice and Behavior* 13(1): 81–97.

Akers, Ronald L. 1985. *Deviant Behavior: A Social Learning Approach*. 3d ed. Belmont, Calif.: Wadsworth.

Albanese, Jay S. 1984. "A Systematic Approach to the Prevention of Shoplifting and Employee Theft." *Journal of Security Administration* 7(1): 23–30.

Alexander, Franz, and William Healy. 1935. *Roots of Crime: Psychoanalytic Studies*. New York: Alfred A. Knopf.

Alexander, Franz, and Hugo Staub. 1962. *The Criminal, The Judge, and The Public: A Psychological Analysis*. New York: Collier.

Anderson, Elijah. 1976. *A Place on the Corner*. Chicago: University of Chicago Press.

Appelbaum, Ann W., and Herbert Klemmer. 1984. "Shoplifting." *Menninger Perspective* (Fall): 16–19.

Arboleda-Florez, J., Helen Durie, and John Costello. "Shoplifting—An Ordinary Crime?" *International Journal of Offender Therapy and Comparative Criminology* 21(3): 201–8.

Asbury, Herbert. 1927. *The Gangs of New York: An Informal History of the Underworld.* New York: Capricorn.

Asch, Solomon E. 1951. "Effects of Group Pressure upon the Modification and Distortion of Judgments." In *Groups, Leadership and Men,* edited by Harold Guetzko. Pittsburgh: Carnegie Press.

Astor, S. D. 1971. "Shoplifting Survey." *Security World* 8(3): 34–35.

Bales, Kevin B. 1982. "Contrast and Complementary in Three Theories of Criminal Behavior." *Deviant Behavior* 3(2): 155–74.

Barmash, Isadore. 1988. "To Catch a Thief (and Enroll Him)." *New York Times,* November 24: D1.

Baumer, Terry L., and Dennis P. Rosenbaum. 1984. *Combatting Retail Theft: Programs and Strategies.* Boston: Butterworth.

Beck, Ester Ann, and Sherwood C. McIntyre. 1977. "MMPI Patterns within a College Population." *Psychological Reports* 41: 1035–40.

Becker, Howard S. 1963. *Outsiders: Studies in the Sociology of Deviance.* New York: Free Press of Glencoe.

Belson, W. A. 1975. *Juvenile Theft: The Causal Factors.* London: Harper & Row.

Bennett, Hilary M. 1968. "Shoplifting in Midtown." *Criminal Law Review* 4: 413–35.

Bernikow, Louise. 1988. "Excuse Me, Miss! Did You Pay for This?" *Mademoiselle* 94(September): 280.

Best, Joel. 1987. "Rhetoric in Claims-Making." *Social Problems* 34(2): 101–21.

Bickman, Leonard. 1975. "Bystander Intervention in a Crime." *Social Psychology* 5(4): 296–302.

Bickman, Leonard, and Susan K. Green. 1977. "Situational Cues and Crime Reporting: Do Signs Make a Difference?" *Journal of Applied Social Psychology* 7(1): 1–18.

Blankenburg, Erhard. 1976. "The Selectivity of Legal Sanctions: An Empirical Investigation of Shoplifting." *Law and Society Review* 11(Fall): 109–30.

Bolen, William H. 1988. *Contemporary Retailing.* Englewood Cliffs, N.J.: Prentice-Hall.

Bollen, Kenneth A., and David P. Phillips. 1982. "Imitative Suicides: A National Study of the Effects of Television News Stories." *American Sociological Review* 47(December): 802–18.

Bowlby, John. 1947. *Forty-four Juvenile Thieves: Their Characters and Homelife.* London: Bailliere, Tindall and Cox.

Brady, J. F., and J. G. Mitchell. 1971. "Shoplifting in Melbourne." *Australian and New Zealand Journal of Criminology* 4(3): 154–62.

Brenton, Myron. 1985. "Women Who Steal." *Cosmopolitan* 189(May): 285.

Breslau, Karen. 1990. "I Want My Wall Back." *Newsweek* (May 28): 33.

Brown, M. Lindsay. 1984. "Five-Finger Discount: A Look at Shoplifting and Retail Security." *USA Today* (November): 64–67.

Bruinsma, G. J. N., C. I. Dessaur, and R. W. J. V. Van Hezewijk. 1984. "Female Criminality in the Netherlands." In *The Incidence of Female Criminality in the Contemporary World*, edited by Freda Adler, pp. 14–63. New York: New York University Press.

Buchalter, Gail. 1990. "I Had to Prove Something." *Parade* (February 18): 19.

Buckle, Abigale, and David P. Farrington. 1984. "An Observational Study of Shoplifting." *British Journal of Criminology* 24(1): 63–73.

Bureau of Justice Statistics: Bulletin. 1984. "The Severity of Crime." Washington, D.C.: U.S. Government Printing Office.

Burgess, Robert L., and Ronald L. Akers. 1966. "A Differential Association-Reinforcement Theory of Criminal Behavior." *Social Problems* 14: 128–47.

Burt, Martha R., and Barbara E. Cohen. 1989. "Differences among Homeless Single Women, Women with Children, and Single Men." *Social Problems* 36(December): 508–24.

Business Week. 1979. "How Shoplifting Is Draining the Economy." October 15: 122–23.

Cameron, Mary Owen. 1964. *The Booster and the Snitch: Department Store Shoplifting*. New York: Free Press of Glencoe.

Campbell, Anne. 1981. *Girl Delinquents*. New York: St. Martin's Press.

Carlson, Ken. 1984. *Unreported Taxable Income from Selected Illegal Activities*. Cambridge, Mass.: Abt Associates.

Carpenter, Cheryl, Barry Glassner, Bruce D. Johnson, and Julia Loughlin. 1988. *Kids, Drugs, and Crime*. Lexington, Mass.: Lexington Books.

Carroll, John, and Frances Weaver. 1986. "Shoplifters' Perceptions of Crime Opportunities: A Process-Tracing Study." In *The Reasoning Criminal*, edited by Derek B. Cornish and Ronald V. Clarke, pp. 19–38. New York: Springer-Verlag.

Cavan, Ruth Shonle, and Theodore N. Ferdinand. 1975. *Juvenile Delinquency*. New York: Lippincott.

Chaiken, Marcia R. 1988. *Street-Level Drug Enforcement: Examining the Issues*. Washington, D.C.: National Institute of Justice.

Chain Store Age Executive. 1988. "Loss Prevention Can Be Profitable." December: 72–73.

———. 1989. "Kiddie City Beefs up Security for New York Outlet." February: 36.

Chambliss, William J. 1984. "Types of Deviance and the Effectiveness of Legal Sanctions." In *Criminal Law in Action*, edited by William J. Chambliss, pp. 425–34. New York: John Wiley & Sons.

Clark, John P., and Richard C. Hollinger. 1983. *Theft by Employees in Work Organizations*. Washington, D.C.: U.S. Government Printing Office.

Cline, Hugh F. 1980. "Criminal Behavior over the Life Span." In *Constancy and Change in Human Development*, edited by Orville G. Brim, Jr., and Jerome Kagan, pp. 641–73. Cambridge, Mass.: Harvard University Press.

Cloward, Richard A., and Lloyd E. Ohlin. 1963. *Delinquency and Opportunity: A Theory of Delinquent Gangs*. New York: Free Press of Glencoe.

Cohen, Albert K. 1955. *Delinquent Boys: The Culture of the Gang*. New York: Free Press of Glencoe.

Cohen, Lawrence, and Rodney Stark. 1974. "Discriminatory Labeling and the Five-Finger Discount: An Empirical Analysis of Differential Shoplifting

Dispositions." *Journal of Research on Crime and Delinquency* 11(January): 25–39.

Cohen, Lawrence E., and Marcus Felson. 1979. "Social Change and Crime Rate Trends." *American Sociological Review* 44(4): 588–607.

Cole, Catherine A. 1989. "Deterrence and Consumer Fraud." *Journal of Retailing* 65(1): 107–20.

Coleman, James William. 1989. *The Criminal Elite: The Sociology of White Collar Crime.* New York: St. Martin's Press.

Cornish, Derek B., and Ronald V. Clarke. 1986. *The Reasoning Criminal: Rational Choice Perspectives.* New York: Springer-Verlag.

Corvallis Gazette-Times. 1990. "Engle Pleads, Then Quits." July 26: B3.

Cox, Dena, Anthony D. Cox, and George P. Moschis. 1990. "When Consumer Behavior Goes Bad: An Investigation of Adolescent Shoplifting." *Journal of Consumer Research* 17(September): 149–59.

Cressey, Donald R. 1971. *Other People's Money.* Belmont, Calif.: Wadsworth.

Cullen, Francis T. 1984. *Rethinking Crime and Deviance Theory: The Emerging of a Structuring Tradition.* Totowa, N.J.: Rowman & Allenheld.

Cunningham, William C., John J. Strauchs, and Clifford W. Van Meter. 1990. *Private Security Trends: 1970 to 2000, The Hallcrest Report II.* Boston: Butterworth-Heinemann.

Cupchic, W., and J. Don Atcheson. 1983. "Shoplifting: An Occasional Crime of the Moral Majority." *Bulletin of the American Academy of Psychiatry and the Law* 11(4): 343–54.

Curran, Debora A. 1984. "Characteristics of the Elderly Shoplifter and the Effects of Sanctions on Recidivism." In *Elderly Criminals,* edited by William Wilbanks and Paul K. H. Kim, pp. 123–41. New York: University Press of America.

Currie, Elliot. 1985. *Confronting Crime: An American Challenge.* New York: Pantheon.

Cusson, Maurice. 1983. *Why Delinquency?* Toronto: University of Toronto Press.

Damon, Janet E. 1988. *Shopaholics: Serious Help for Addicted Spenders.* Los Angeles: Price Stern Sloan.

Davis, Mellissa G., Richard J. Lundman, and Ramiro Martinez, Jr. 1991. "Private Corporate Justice: Store Police, Shoplifters, and Civil Recovery." *Social Problems* 38(August): 395–411.

Dertke, M. C., L. A. Penner, and K. Ulrich. 1974. "Observer's Reporting of Shoplifting as a Function of Thief's Race and Sex." *Journal of Social Psychology* 8: 377–83.

Dowling, Claudia. 1988. "Shoplifting: Bess Myerson's Arrest Highlights a Multimillion-Dollar Problem That Many Stores Won't Talk About." *Life* (August): 32.

Durkheim, Emile. 1951. *Suicide: A Study in Sociology.* New York: Free Press of Glencoe.

Edwards, Loren E. 1970. *Shoplifting and Shrinkage Protection for Stores.* Springfield, Ill.: Charles C. Thomas.

El-Dirghami, Amin. 1974. "Shoplifting among Students." *Journal of Retailing* 50(Fall): 33–42.

Elliott, Delbert S., David Huizinga, and Suzanne S. Ageton. 1985. *Explaining Delinquency and Drug Use*. Beverly Hills: Sage.

Emerson, Robert M. 1991. "Case Processing and Interorganizational Knowledge: Detecting the 'Real Reasons' for Referrals." *Social Problems* 38(2): 198–212.

Erickson, Maynard L. 1973. "Group Violations and Official Delinquency: The Group Hazard Hypothesis." *Criminology* 11: 127–60.

Erickson, Maynard L., and Lamar T. Empey. 1963. "Court Records, Undetected Delinquency, and Decision Making." *Journal of Criminal Law, Criminology, and Police Science* 54: 456–69.

Erickson, Maynard L., and Gary F. Jensen. 1977. "Delinquency Is Still Group Behavior! Toward Revitalizing the Group Premise in the Sociology of Deviance." *Journal of Criminal Law and Criminology* 68(2): 262–72.

Erman, M. David, and Richard J. Lundman. 1987. *Corporate and Governmental Deviance*. New York: Oxford University Press.

Espinoza, Douglas C. 1989. "Shoplifters No Sale." *Security Management* (May): 65–69.

Ewen, Stuart. 1976. *Captains of Consciousness: Advertising and the Social Roots of the Consumer Culture*. New York: McGraw-Hill.

Faria, Anthony J. 1977. "Minimizing Shoplifting Losses: Some Practical Guidelines." *Journal of Small Business Management* 15(October): 37–43.

Farnsworth, Margaret, and Michael J. Leiber. 1989. "Strain Theory Revisited." *American Sociological Review* 54(April): 263–74.

Farrell, Jeff. 1990. "Crimes of Style: Urban Graffiti and the Politics of Deviance." Paper presented at the annual meeting of the Academy of Criminal Justice Sciences, Denver, 13–17 March.

Farrell, Katheleen L. 1985. *Shoplifting: The Antishoplifting Guidebook*. New York: Praeger.

Faupel, Charles E. 1986. "Heroin Use, Street Crime, and the 'Main Hustle': Implications for the Validity of Official Crime Data." *Deviant Behavior* 7(1): 31–45.

Faupel, Charles E., and Carl B. Klockars. 1987. "Drugs-Crime Connections: Elaborations from Life Histories of Hard-Core Heroin Addicts." *Social Problems* 34(February): 54–68.

Federal Bureau of Investigation. 1975. *Crime in the United States, 1974: Uniform Crime Reports*. Washington, D.C.: U.S. Government Printing Office.

———. 1990. *Crime in the United States, 1989: Uniform Crime Reports*. Washington D.C.: U.S. Government Printing Office.

Fedler, Fred, and Bert Pryor. 1984. "An Equity Theory Explanation of Bystanders' Reactions to Shoplifting." *Psychological Reports* 54: 746.

Fein, Sherman E., and Arthur M. Maskell. 1975. *Selected Cases on the Law of Shoplifting*. Springfield, Ill.: Charles C. Thomas.

Feinberg, Gary. 1984a. "Profile of the Elderly Shoplifter." In *Elderly Criminals*, edited by Evelyn S. Newman, Donald J. Newman, Mindy L. Gewirtz, and associates, pp. 35–50. Cambridge, Mass.: Oelgeschlager, Gunn & Hain.

———. 1984b. "White Haired Offenders: An Emergent Social Problem." In *Elderly Criminals*, edited by William Wilbanks and Paul K. H. Kim, pp. 83–122. New York: University Press of America.

Feuerverger, Andrey, and Clifford D. Shearing. 1982. "An Analysis of the Prosecution of Shoplifters." *Criminology* 20(2): 273–89.

Fisher, Bonnie. 1991. "A Neighborhood Business Area Is Hurting: Crime, Fear of Crime, and Disorders Take Their Toll." *Crime and Delinquency* 37(3): 363–73.

Flanagan, Timothy J., and Kathleen Maguire, eds. 1990. *Sourcebook of Criminal Justice Statistics 1989*. Washington, D.C.: U.S. Government Printing Office.

French, Warren A., Melvin R. Crask, and Fred H. Mader. 1984. "Retailer's Assessment of the Shoplifting Problem." *Journal of Retailing* 60(4): 108–14.

Fyfe, James J. 1984. "Police Dilemmas in Processing Elderly Offenders." In *Elderly Criminals*, edited by Evelyn S. Newman, Donald J. Newman, Mindy L. Gewirtz, and associates, pp. 97–111. Cambridge, Mass.: Oelgeschlager, Gunn and Hain.

Gelfand, Donna M., Donald P. Hartman, Patrice Walder, and Brent Page. 1973. "Who Reports Shoplifters? A Field-Experimental Study." *Journal of Personality and Social Psychology* 25(2): 276–85.

Gibbens, T. C. N. 1981. "Shoplifting." *British Journal of Psychiatry* 138: 346–47.

Gibbons, Don C. 1985. "The Assumption of the Efficacy of Middle-Range Explanations: Typologies." In *Theoretical Methods in Criminology*, edited by Robert F. Meier, pp. 151–76. Beverly Hills: Sage.

Goffman, Erving. 1959. *The Presentation of Self in Everyday Life*. Garden City, N.Y.: Doubleday Anchor.

———. 1967. "Where the Action Is." In *Interaction Ritual: Essays on Face-to-Face Behavior*, pp. 149–270. Garden City, N.Y.: Anchor Books.

Gold, Martin. 1970. *Delinquent Behavior in an American City*. Belmont, Calif.: Brooks/Cole.

Gottfredson, Michael, and Travis Hirschi. 1990. *A General Theory of Crime*. Stanford: Stanford University Press.

Griffin, Roger. 1988. *25th Annual Report: Shoplifting in Supermarkets*. Van Nuys, Calif.: Commercial Service Systems.

Grosswirth, Marvin. 1981. "When Grandma Is a Thief." *50 Plus* (November): 74–77.

Group 4. 1972. "Are Britons Four Times More Honest Than Yankees?" Paper submitted to the Home Office Working Party on Internal Shop Security.

Groves, W. Bryan, and Michael J. Lynch. 1990. "Reconciling Structural and Subjective Approaches to the Study of Crime." *Journal of Research in Crime and Delinquency* 27(4): 348–75.

Guffey, Hugh J., Jr., James R. Harris, and J. Ford Laumer. 1979. "Shoppers' Attitudes toward Shoplifting and Shoplifting Preventive Devices." *Journal of Retailing* 55(3): 75–89.

Gusfield, Joseph P. 1989. "Constructing the Ownership of Social Problems: Fun and Profit in the Welfare State." *Social Problems* 36(2): 431–43.

Hagan, John, and Bill McCarthy. 1992. "Streetlife and Delinquency: The Significance of a Missing Population." *British Journal of Sociology* (forthcoming).

Hakeem, Michael. 1985. "The Assumption That Crime Is a Product of Individual

Characteristics: A Prime Example from Psychiatry." In *Theoretical Methods in Criminology*, edited by Robert F. Meier, pp. 197–222. Beverly Hills: Sage.

Hanson, Bill, George Beschner, James M. Walters, and Elliot Bovelle, eds. 1985. *Life with Heroin: Voices from the Inner City*. Lexington, Mass.: Lexington Books.

Hawkins, Richard, and Gary Tiedeman. 1975. *The Creation of Deviance*. Columbus, Ohio: Charles E. Merrill.

Herman, Nancy. 1987. "Mixed Nutters and Looney Tuners: The Emergence, Development, Nature, and Functions of Two Informal, Deviant Subcultures of Chronic, Ex-Psychiatric Patients." *Deviant Behavior* 8(3): 235–58.

Hiew, Chok C. 1981. "Prevention of Shoplifting: A Community Action Approach." *Canadian Journal of Criminology* 23(1): 57–73.

Hills, Stuart. 1987. *Corporate Violence: Injury and Death for Profit*. Savage, Md.: Rowan & Littlefield.

Hindlelang, Michael J. 1974. "Decisions of Shoplifting Victims to Invoke the Criminal Justice Process." *Social Problems* 21(April): 580–93.

Hindelang, Michael J., Travis Hirschi, and Joseph G. Weis. 1981. *Measuring Delinquency*. Beverly Hills: Sage.

Hirschi, Travis. 1969. *Causes of Delinquency*. Berkeley: University of California Press.

Hoffman, Abbie. 1971. *Steal This Book*. New York: Grove Press.

Inciardi, James A. 1980. "Women, Heroin, and Property Crime." In *Women, Crime, and Justice*, edited by Susan K. Datesman and Frank R. Scarpitti, pp. 214–21. New York: Oxford University Press.

Jarvis, Graham, and Howard Parker., 1989. "Young Heroin Users and Crime: How Do the 'New Users' Finance Their Habits?" *British Journal of Criminology* 29(2): 175–85.

Jet. 1989. "Ex-Mayor Stokes Admits Taking Store Screwdriver." (January): 4.

Johnson, Bruce D., Paul J. Goldstein, Edward Preble, James Schmeidler, Douglas S. Lipton, Barry Spunt, and Thomas Miller. 1985. *Taking Care of Business: The Economics of Crime by Heroin Abusers*. Lexington, Mass.: Lexington Books.

Johnson, Scott Lee, Robert Sommer, and Victor Martino, 1985. "Consumer Behavior at Bulk Food Bins." *Journal of Consumer Research* 12(June): 114–17.

Johnston, Lloyd D., Jerald G. Bachman, and Patrick M. O'Malley. 1977–1986. *Monitoring the Future*. Ann Arbor: Institute for Social Research.

Judges, A. F. 1930. *The Elizabethan Underworld*. London: G. Routledge & Sons.

Juvenile Justice Digest. 1987. "Modern-day Fagin Leading Child Shoplifters, Police Say." 15(9): 9.

Kallis, M. Jeffery, and Dinoo J. Vanier. 1985. "Consumer Shoplifting: Orientations and Deterrents." *Journal of Criminal Justice* 13: 459–73.

Kaplan, Louise J. 1991. *Female Perversions: The Temptations of Emma Bovary*. New York: Doubleday.

Katz, Jack. 1988. *Seductions of Crime: Moral and Sensual Attractions in Doing Evil*. New York: Basic Books.

Klapp, Orrin E. 1969. *Collective Search for Identity*. New York: Rinehart and Winston.

Klemke, Lloyd W. 1978a. "Does Apprehension for Shoplifting Amplify or Terminate Shoplifting Activity?" *Law and Society Review* 12(Spring): 391–403.
———. 1978b. "Reassessment of the Adolescent Crime Wave Model." *California Sociologist* 1(Summer): 183–92.
———. 1982a. "Exploring Juvenile Shoplifting." *Sociology and Social Research* 67(October): 59–75.
———. 1982b. "Reassessment of Cameron's Apprehension-Termination of Shoplifting Finding." *California Sociologist* 5(Winter): 88–96.
———. 1988. "Deviant Modes of Adaptations to a Deviant Involvement." *Deviant Behavior* 9(3): 225–40.
Klemke, Lloyd W., and Gary H. Tiedeman. 1981. "Toward an Understanding of False Accusation: The Pure Case of Deviant Labeling." *Deviant Behavior* 2(3): 261–87.
Klentz, Bonnel, and Arthur L. Beaman. 1981. "The Effects of Type of Information and Method of Dissemination on the Reporting of a Shoplifter." *Journal of Applied Social Psychology* 11(1): 64–82.
Klockars, Carl B. 1974. *The Professional Fence*. New York: Free Press.
Klokis, Holly. 1985. "Confessions of an Ex-Shoplifter." *Chain Store Age Executive* (February): 15–18.
Kluckholm, Clyde, and Henry A. Murray. 1944. "Culture and Personality: A Conceptual Scheme." *American Anthropologist* 46: 1–29.
Kolman, Anita Sue, and Claudia Wasserman. 1991. "Theft Groups for Women: A Cry for Help." *Federal Probation* 55(1): 48–54.
Kopecky, Gini. 1980. "Shoplifting: Why Women Who Have Everything Steal." *Mademoiselle* (December): 156.
Kornhauser, Ruth Rosner. 1978. *Sources of Delinquency: An Appraisal of Analytic Models*. Chicago: University of Chicago Press.
Kowalski, Gregory S., and Charles E. Faupel. 1990. "Heroin Use, Crime, and the 'Main Hustle'." *Deviant Behavior* 11(1): 1–16.
Kraut, Robert E. 1976. "Deterrent and Definitional Influences on Shoplifting." *Social Problems* 25(February): 358–68.
Lab, Steven P. 1988. *Crime Prevention: Approaches, Practices, and Evaluations*. Cincinnati: Anderson Publishing.
Latané, Bibb, and John M. Darley. 1970. *The Unresponsive Bystander: Why Doesn't He Help?* New York: Appleton-Century-Crofts.
Lemert, Edwin. 1951. *Social Pathology: A Systematic Approach to the Theory of Sociopathic Behavior*. New York: McGraw-Hill.
Lesser, Ellen. 1989. *The Shoplifter's Apprentice*. New York: Simon and Schuster.
Lex, Barbara W. 1990. "Narcotics Addicts' Hustling Strategies: Creation and Manipulation of Ambiguity." *Journal of Contemporary Ethnography* 18(4): 388–415.
Liska, Allen E. 1971. "Aspirations, Expectations and Delinquency, Stress and Additional Models." *Sociological Quarterly* 12: 99–107.
Lombroso, Caesar, and William Ferrero. 1898. *The Female Offender*. New York: D. Appleton.
Lundman, Richard J. 1978. "Shoplifting and Police Referral: A Reexamination." *Journal of Criminal Law and Criminology* 69(3): 395–401.

McCarthy, Bill, and John Hagan. 1991. "Homelessness: A Criminogenic Situation." *British Journal of Criminology* 31(4): 393–410.

Macdonald, John M. 1980. *Burglary and Theft*. Springfield, Ill.: Charles C. Thomas.

McNees, M. Patrick, Daniel S. Egli, Rebecca S. Marshall, John F. Schnelle, and Todd R. Risley. 1976. "Shoplifting Prevention: Providing Information through Signs." *Journal of Applied Behavioral Analysis* 9(4): 399–405.

Maguire, Kathleen, and Timothy J. Flanagan, eds. 1991. *Sourcebook of Criminal Justice Statistics—1990*. Washington, D.C.: U.S. Government Printing Office.

Mahew, Henry. 1968. *London Labour and the London Poor*, Vol. 4. New York: Dover Publications.

Marks, D. A. 1975. "Retail Store Security in Ireland." *Top Security* (September): 204–6.

Marx, Gary, 1988. *Undercover: Police Surveillance in America*. Berkeley: University of California Press.

Mawson, Anthony R. 1987. *Transient Criminality: A Model of Stress-Induced Crime*. New York: Praeger.

May, David. 1978. "Juvenile Shoplifters and the Organization of Store Security: A Case Study in the Social Construction of Delinquency." *International Journal of Criminology and Penology* 6: 137–60.

Mead, George H. 1934. *Mind, Self, and Society*. Chicago: University of Chicago Press.

Meier, Robert F., ed. 1984. *Major Forms of Crime*. Beverly Hills: Sage.

Merton, Robert K. 1938. "Social Structure and Anomie." *American Sociological Review* 3: 672–82.

Miller, Eleanor M. 1986. *Street Woman*. Philadelphia: Temple University Press.

Miller, Gale. 1978. *Odd Jobs: The World of Deviant Work*. Englewood Cliffs, N.J.: Prentice-Hall.

Minerbrook, Scott. 1988. "A Face-Off with Racism: In a Manhattan Train Station, Grappling with the Tricky Questions of Prejudice and Race Relations." *U.S. News & World Report* 105(August 22): 57.

Minor, W. William. 1981. "Techniques of Neutralization: A Reconceptualization and Empirical Examination." *Journal of Research in Crime and Delinquency* (July): 295–318.

Minor, W. William, and Joseph Harry. 1982. "Deterrent and Experimental Effects in Perceptual Deterrence Research." *Journal of Research in Crime and Delinquency* 19(2): 190–203.

Mitchell, Richard G., Jr. 1984. "Alienation and Deviance: Strain Theory Reconsidered." *Social Inquiry* 54(3): 336–45.

Moak, Gary S., Ben Zimmer, and Elliot M. Stein. 1988. "Clinical Perspectives on Elderly First-Offender Shoplifters." *Hospital and Community Psychiatry* 39(June): 648–51.

Moore, Richard H. 1983. "College Shoplifters: Rebuttal of Beck and McIntyre." *Psychological Reports* 53: 1111–16.

———. 1984. "Shoplifting in Middle America: Patterns and Motivational Correlates." *International Journal of Offender Therapy and Comparative Criminology* 28(1): 53–64.

Moschis, George P. 1987. *Consumer Socialization: A Life-Cycle Perspective*. Lexington, Mass.: Lexington Books.

Murphy, Daniel J. I. 1986. *Customers and Thieves: An Ethnography of Shoplifting*. Aldershot, England: Gower.

Neustatter, W. Lindesay. 1954. "The Psychology of Shoplifting." *Medico-Legal Journal* 22(4): 118–30.

Nimick, Ellen H. 1990. "Juvenile Court Property Cases." *OJJDP Update on Statistics* (November): 1–5.

Nye, F. Ivan. 1958. *Family Relationships and Delinquent Behavior*. New York: John Wiley & Sons.

O'Brien, Patricia. 1983. "Bourgeois Women and Theft." *Journal of Social History* 17(Fall): 65–77.

O'Guinn, Thomas C., and Ronald J. Faber. 1989. "Compulsive Buying: A Phenomenological Exploration." *Journal of Consumer Research* 16(September): 147–57.

Oregon Law Enforcement Data System. 1989. *Report of Criminal Offenses and Arrests 1988*. Salem, Oreg.: Law Enforcement Data System.

Osgood, Wayne D., Patrick M. O'Malley, Gerald G. Bachman, and Lloyd D. Johnston. 1989. "Time Trends and Age Trends in Arrests and Self-Reported Illegal Behavior." *Criminology* 27(3): 389–415.

Paikert, Charles. 1982. "Joblessness, Recession Aggravate Security Woes." *Chain Store Age Executive* (April): 35.

Patternoster, Raymond. 1989. "Absolute and Restrictive Deterrence in a Panel Study of Youth: Explaining the Onset, Persistence/Desistence, and Frequency of Delinquent Offending." *Social Problems* 36(3): 289–309.

Patterson, G. R. 1980. "Children Who Steal." In *Understanding Crime: Current Theory and Research*, edited by Travis Hirschi and Michael Gottfredson, pp. 73–90. Beverly Hills: Sage.

Phillips, David P. 1974. "The Influence of Suggestion on Suicide: Substantive and Theoretical Implications of the Werther Effect." *American Sociological Review* 39(3): 340–54.

Piliavin, Irving, Rosemary Gartner, Craig Thornton, and Ross Matsueda. 1986. "Crime, Deterrence, and Choice." *American Sociological Review* 51(1): 101–19.

Pousner, Michael. 1988. "Women Who Shoplift." *Cosmopolitan* (April): 162.

Prus, Robert, and Styllianoss Irini. 1980. *Hookers, Rounders, and Desk Clerks: The Social Organization of the Hotel Community*. Salem, Wis.: Sheffield.

Purpura, Philip P. 1984. *Security Loss and Prevention*. Boston: Butterworth.

Ray, JoAnn. 1987. "Every Twelfth Shopper: Who Shoplifts and Why?" *Social Casework* 68 (April): 234–39.

Ray, JoAnn, and Katherine H. Briar. 1988. "Economic Motivators for Shoplifting." *Journal of Sociology and Social Welfare* 15(4): 177–89.

Rettig, Richard P., Manual J. Torres, and Gerald R. Garrett. 1977. *Manny: A Criminal-Addict's Story*. Boston: Houghton Mifflin.

Richards, Pamela, Richard Berk, and Brenda Forster. 1979. *Crime as Play: Delinquency in a Middle Class Suburb*. Cambridge, Mass.: Ballinger.

Robin, Gerald D. 1963. "Patterns of Department Store Shoplifting." *Crime and Delinquency* 9(April): 163–72.

Rook, Dennis W. 1987. "The Buying Impulse." *Journal of Consumer Research* 14(September): 189–98.

Rosenberg, Bernard, and Harry Silverstein. 1969. *The Varieties of Delinquent Experience.* Waltham, Mass.: Blaisdell.

Rossi, Peter H., Christine E. Bose, and Richard E. Berk. 1974. "The Seriousness of Crimes: Normative Structure and Individual Differences." *American Sociological Review* 39(April): 224–37.

Rouke, Fabian L. 1955. "Shoplifting: Its Symbolic Motivation." *Journal of Social Therapy* 1: 95–99.

Royse, David, and Steven A. Buck. 1991. "Evaluating a Diversion Program for First-Time Shoplifters." *Journal of Offender Rehabilitation* 17(1/2): 139–50.

Rubin, Jerry. 1970. *Do It: Scenarios of the Revolution.* New York: Simon and Schuster.

Sacco, Vincent F. 1985. "Shoplifting Prevention: The Role of Communication-Based Intervention Strategies." *Canadian Journal of Criminology* 27(1): 15–29.

Saltzman, Linda, Raymond Patternoster, and Waldo G. Chirocos. 1982. "Deterrent and Experiential Effects: The Problem of Causal Order in Perceptual Deterrence Research." *Journal of Research in Crime and Delinquency* 19(July): 172–89.

Schafer, Walter E., and Kenneth Polk. 1967. "Delinquency and the Schools." In *Task Force Report: Juvenile Delinquency and Youth Crime,* edited by The President's Commission on Law Enforcement and Administration of Justice, pp. 222–77. Washington, D.C.: U.S. Government Printing Office.

Scheff, Thomas. 1966. *Being Mentally Ill: A Sociological Theory.* Chicago: Aldine.

Schlueter, Gregory R., Francis C. O'Neal, JoAnn Hickey, and Gloria L. Seiler. 1989. "Rational vs. Nonrational Shoplifting Types: The Implications for Loss Prevention." *International Journal of Offender Therapy and Comparative Criminology* 33(3): 227–39.

Schur, Edwin M. 1969. *Our Criminal Society.* Englewood Cliffs, N.J.: Prentice-Hall.

———. 1971. *Labeling Deviant Behavior.* New York: Harper & Row.

Schwartz, Sanford, and Herman V. Wood. 1991. "Clinical Assessment and Intervention with Shoplifters." *Social Work* 36(May): 234–8.

Schwendinger, Herman, and Julia Siegel Schwendinger. 1985. *Adolescent Subcultures and Delinquency.* New York: Praeger.

Shapland, J. 1978. "Self-Reported Delinquency in Boys Aged 11 to 14." *British Journal of Criminology* 18(3): 255–65.

Sharff, Jagna Wojcicka. 1981. "Free Enterprise and the Ghetto Family." *Psychology Today* (March): 41–48.

Shaw, Clifford R. 1930. *The Jack-Roller: A Delinquent Boy's Own Story.* Chicago: University of Chicago Press.

———. 1931. *The Natural History of a Delinquent Career.* Chicago: University of Chicago Press.

Sherman, Lawrence W. 1990. "Crackdowns." In *Crime and Justice: A Review of Research,* Vol. 12, edited by Michael Tonry and James Q. Wilson. Chicago: University of Chicago Press.

Sherman, Lawrence W., and Patrick R. Gartin. 1986. "Differential Recidivism:

A Field Experiment on the Specific Sanction Effects of Arrest for Shoplifting." Crime Control Institute Report. Washington, D.C.: Crime Control Institute.

Short, James F., Ramon Rivera, and Roy A. Tennyson. 1965. "Perceived Opportunities, Gang Membership and Delinquency." *American Sociological Review* 30: 56–67.

Simon, David R., and D. Stanley Eitzen. 1982. *Elite Deviance*. Boston: Allyn and Bacon.

Sloane, Leonard. 1991. "Devices That Try to Outwit Shoplifters." *New York Times: Consumer's World* (August 24): 20.

Smith, Douglas A., and Patrick R. Gartin. 1989. "Specifying Specific Deterrence." *American Sociological Review* 54(1): 94–107.

Snodgrass, Jon. 1982. *The Jack-Roller at Seventy: A Fifty Year Follow-up*. Lexington, Mass.: Lexington Books.

Snow, David A., Susan G. Baker, and Leon Anderson. 1989. "Criminality and Homeless Men: An Empirical Assessment." *Social Problems* 36(December): 532–47.

Spergle, Irving. 1964. *Racketville, Slumtown, and Haulberg: An Exploratory Study of Delinquent Subcultures*. Chicago: University of Chicago Press.

Steffensmeier, Darrell J. 1986. *The Fence: In the Shadow of Two Worlds*. Totowa, N.J.: Rowman & Littlefield.

Steffensmeier, Darrell J., and Renée Hoffman Steffensmeier. 1977. "Who Reports Shoplifters? Research Continuities and Further Developments." *Journal of Criminology and Penology* 5: 79–95.

Steffensmeier, Darrell J., and Robert T. Terry. 1973. "Deviance and Respectability: An Observational Study of Reactions to Shoplifting." *Social Forces* 51: 417–26.

Sutherland, Edwin H., and Donald R. Cressey. 1970. *Principles of Criminology*. Philadelphia: J. B. Lippincott.

Sutter, Alan G. 1969. "Worlds of Drug Use on the Street Scene." In *Delinquency, Crime, and Social Process*, edited by Donald R. Cressey and David A. Ward. New York: Harper and Row.

Sykes, Gresham M., and David Matza. 1957. "Techniques of Neutralization: A Theory of Delinquency." *American Sociological Review* 22(6): 664–70.

Tannenbaum, Frank. 1938. *Crime and the Community*. Boston: Ginn.

Tauber, Edward M. 1972. "Why Do People Shop?" *Journal of Marketing* 36(October): 46–59.

Taylor, L. B., Jr. 1982. "Shoplifting: When 'Honest' Women Steal." *Ladies Home Journal* 99(January): 88.

The Oregonian. 1991. "Leaders Admit Shoplifting Role." May 17: 22.

The Register-Guard. 1991. "Actress' Shoplifting Arrest Sparks Fans' Offers of Help." August 3: 2a.

Thorsell, Bernard A., and Lloyd W. Klemke. 1972. "The Labeling Process: Reinforcement and Deterrent." *Law & Society Review* 6(3): 393–404.

Thrasher, Frederick M. 1927. *The Gang: A Study of 1,313 Gangs in Chicago*. Chicago: University of Chicago Press.

Thurber, Steven, and Mark Snow. 1980. "Signs May Prompt Antisocial Behavior." *Journal of Social Psychology* 112: 309–10.

Time. 1986. "The Case of the $99 Raincoat: Iran's UN Ambassador Accused of Shoplifting." June 2: 27.

Tittle, Charles R. 1980. *Sanctions and Social Deviance: The Question of Deterrence*. New York: Praeger.

Tittle, Charles R., and Alan A. Rowe. 1973. "Certainty of Arrest and Crime Rates: A Further Test of the Deterrence Hypothesis." *Social Forces* 52: 455–62.

Tooley, Jo Ann. 1989. "Smugglers at the Supermarket." *U.S. News & World Report* (March 13): 73.

Tsiantar, Dody. 1989. "Big Brother at the Mall: Retailers Go High Tech in the War on Shoplifters." *Newsweek* (July 3): 44.

Tunnell, Kenneth D. 1992. *Choosing Crime: The Criminal Calculus of Property Offenders*. Chicago: Nelson-Hall Publishers.

Turner, Castellano B., and Sheldon Cashdan. 1988. "Perception of College Students' Motives for Shoplifting." *Psychological Reports* 62: 855–62.

U.S. News & World Report. 1986. "Capitols' Needy Seek Relief." (December 1): 5.

Valentine, Bettylou. 1978. *Hustling and Other Hard Work*. New York: Free Press.

Van Den Hagg, Ernst. 1975. *Punishing Criminals: Concerning a Very Old and Painful Question*. New York: Basic Books.

Veblen, Thorstein. 1953. *The Theory of the Leisure Class: An Economic Study of Institutions*. New York: New American Library.

Walker, Samuel. 1985. *Sense and Nonsense about Crime: A Policy Guide*. Monterey, Calif.: Brooks/Cole.

Walsh, D. P. 1978. *Shoplifting: Controlling a Major Crime*. New York: Holmes and Meier.

Walsh, Marilyn E. 1977. *The Fence: A New Look at the World of Property Theft*. Westport, Conn.: Greenwood Press.

Warr, Mark. 1989. "What Is the Perceived Seriousness of Crimes?" *Criminology* 27(4): 795–821.

Weiner, Norman L. 1970. "The Teen-Age Shoplifter: A Microcosmic View of Middle-Class Delinquency." In *Observations of Deviance*, edited by Jack D. Douglas, pp. 213–17. New York: Random House.

Wiatrowski, Michael, David Griswold, and Mary K. Roberts.1981. "Social Control Theory and Delinquency." *American Sociological Review* 46: 525–41.

Wiessler, David A. 1982. "Surge in Petty Theft: Symptom of Hard Times." *U.S. News & World Report* (July 19): 50.

Wilbanks, William. 1984. "The Elderly Offender: Sex and Race Variations in Frequency and Pattern." In *Elderly Criminals*, edited by William Wilbanks and Paul K. H. Kim, p. 41–51. New York: University Press of America.

Wilkes, Robert E. 1978. "Fraudulent Behavior by Consumers." *Journal of Marketing* (October): 67–75.

Wilkins, Leslie T. 1965. *Social Deviance: Social Policy, Action, and Research*. Englewood Cliffs, N.J.: Tavistock.

Wilkinson, Karen. 1980. "The Broken Home and Delinquent Behavior." In *Understanding Crime: Current Theory and Research*, edited by Travis Hirschi and Michael Gottfredson, pp. 21–41. Beverly Hills: Sage.

Williams, Hubert, Brian Forst, and Edwin Hamilton. 1987. "Stop! You Should Arrest That Person." *Security Management* (September): 52–57.

Williams, Richard, and J. Thomas Dalby. 1986. "Benzodiazepines and Shoplifting." *International Journal of Offender Therapy and Comparative Criminology* 30(1): 35–39.

Williams, Terry, and William Kornblum. 1985. *Growing Up Poor.* Lexington, Mass.: Lexington Books.

Winfree, L. Thomas, Christine S. Sellers, Patricia Michelle Duncan, Gabrielle Kelly, Larry E. Williams, and Lawrence Clinton. 1989. "Returning to Delinquency: Factors Affecting the Survivorship of Juvenile Shoplifters." *Juvenile & Family Court Journal* 40: 49–62.

Witkin, Georgia. 1988. *Quick Fixes and Small Comforts: How Every Woman Can Resist Those Irresistible Urges.* New York: Villard Books.

Won, George, and George Yamamoto. 1968. "Social Structure and Deviant Behavior: A Study of Shoplifting." *Sociology and Social Research* 53: 44–55.

Yates, Elizabeth. 1986. "The Influence of Psycho-Social Factors on Non-Sensical Shoplifting." *International Journal of Offender Therapy and Comparative Criminology* 30(3): 203–11.

Ziolko, H. V. 1988. "Bulimia and Kleptomania: Psychodynamics of Compulsive Eating and Stealing." In *Bulimia: Psychoanalytic Treatment and Theory,* edited by Harvey J. Schwartz, pp. 523–34. Madison, Conn.: International University Press.

Zuckerman, Marvin. 1978. "The Search for High Sensation." *Psychology Today* (February): 39–46.

SUBJECT INDEX

NAME INDEX

About the Author

LLOYD W. KLEMKE has been involved in research on shoplifting for over 15 years. He is Professor of Sociology at Oregon State University, where his areas of specialization include deviant behavior and juvenile delinquency.